THE GOSPEL
ACCORDING TO SAM

THE GOSPEL ACCORDING TO

*Animal Stories
for the Soul*

WILLIAM MILLER

Church Publishing
NEW YORK

Church Publishing
19 East 34th Street
New York, NY 10016
www.churchpublishing.org

A catalog record for this book is available from the Library of Congress

ISBN 13: 978-1-59627-274-3 (pbk)

Printed in the United States of America

For Sam

Contents

Part Three
NEW DOG, OLD TRICKS

$\mathcal{A}$cknowledgments

I am grateful to my parents, Bill and Evelyn, for teaching me that stories communicate eternal truth and that God knows my name. I also appreciate my surrogate parents, Rosemary and Hank, for making me aware of the abundance of creation and the sacramental sustenance found in cookies and beer.

A host of friends, teachers, travel buddies, mentors, and exes have made life interesting, enlightening, and joyful. I have been blessed by extraordinary communities of open people at St. James Episcopal Church in Austin and Trinity Episcopal Church in Houston. Thank you for letting me be me, even in the pulpit and behind the altar.

Bill Broyles and Peter Lewis provided early affirmation that I just might be a writer. Ellen Whittier and Eileen O'Brien miraculously edited my scribbled hieroglyphics and maintained an appreciative sense of humor. Nancy and Pete Etheridge graciously opened their homes to man and beasts. Carol Barnwell has been supportive in many ways, and Susan Erdey and all the folks at Seabury have embraced my quirkiness with unrestrained enthusiasm.

Rachel Burrow continues to speak to me, laugh at my jokes, and even scratch my head on occasion. For bringing the boys into my life and for looking a lot like Barbie in the process, she is hereby awarded the Spandex Prize for Literary Inspiration.

To Episcopalians everywhere, thanks for being the kind of people with whom I can pray and party! It's been a wild ride and grace-filled adventure. I am grateful for every meaningful moment and for all of God's creatures who have so enriched my life. I know I've seen more than my share of tails along the way, but none more inspiring than those belonging to Sam and Jack, my faithful Airedales. Who knew that a furry ass could be such a beautiful thing? It gives me great hope.

The Feast Day of Saint Irenaeus
June 28, 2005

The glory of God is the human being fully alive.
Saint Irenaeus

Prologue

You cannot tell people what to do, you can only tell them parables.
W. H. AUDEN

I will open my mouth in a parable;
I will declare the mysteries of ancient times.
PSALM 78:2

Jesus told the crowds all these things in parables;
without a parable he told them nothing.
MATTHEW 13:34

Tell me a story—NOW!
CHRIS MILLER (my nephew), age four

I am not as smart as Auden, as insightful as the psalmist, as spiritual as Jesus, or as subtle as my nephew Chris, but I do have a story to tell—several stories, actually. They are stories of varied lengths, unpredictable outcomes, and questionable characters. There are tales about catastrophes and chaos, faithfulness and futility, blessing and curse, struggle and survival. You will read of pets and pigs, relationships and rabbits, cowboys and communion. You will meet such creatures as one-legged birds, deep-diving whales, and hard-working yaks. You will encounter edible bugs, dangerous bulls, and basking turtles, not to mention more than a few mules. Rooted in the real world, these stories are true, and, as such, hopefully contain some measure of The Truth.

When I was a young child in Mrs. Mylie's Sunday school class, she once asked us, "What is a parable?" I was going to answer, "It's a story about stuff Jesus saw," but before I could respond, Brad Taylor's hand shot up in the air. "A parable is an earthly story with a heavenly meaning," Brad recited piously. Mrs. Mylie smiled and said, "That's absolutely right." After all, Brad's father was the preacher, so if anyone would know, it would be Brad. None of us knew exactly what that phrase "earthly story with a heavenly meaning" actually meant, but it sure sounded good, so we repeated it to future Sunday school teachers for the next six years, getting it "right" every time!

Some years later I'm rarely getting it right, but I'm finally starting to get it. It turns out that my initial response to Mrs. Mylie's question was not too far off track. Earthly stories are about real people with real problems in real places. We live and move and have our being in the natural world, and all Creation speaks to us poignantly of God's longing and desire. Heavenly meanings touch our souls, sustain our spirits, enliven our minds, inspire our imaginations, and spark our dreams. Thus, parables—which contain both levels of reality—arise simply from the stuff of our existence: what we see, hear, taste, smell, touch, and feel.

At the same time, such stories seem to draw us beyond the here and now, above our limitations and toward that which we might become. The stories of the created bear the imprint of the Creator. If you need a hifalutin' theological term to express this concept, try *incarnation*. In the Christian tradition, "incarnation" means that when God wanted to ultimately communicate with us, God put flesh on the Word. The Word became human, earthly, physical; it dwelt among us, right here where all of us live. God still comes to us and reveals divinity in the common, ordinary, earthly material of our lives: loyal dogs, faithful friends, tasty treats, foibles, sins, triumphs, graces, adventures, and misadventures. The divine is in the details of our lives. God still dwells in the Word and in the world, in the stories we live out each day.

There is no need to establish a false dichotomy between the earthly and heavenly. Both are manifestations of the same God. The true parable reveals that the sacred and secular are Siamese twins who refuse to be separated. Whether soulful or shadowy, good or bad, beautiful or ugly, the stories we share reveal glimpses of God. And if within these tellings and retellings we contradict ourselves, it does not invalidate their truth. It simply affirms our largeness and the largeness of the One who made us.

Most biblical scholars agree that there are two creation stories in the book of Genesis. In the first creation story, God plays with the lighting and set for the first four days. After getting the stage sorted out, it's time to introduce the characters. Interestingly enough, God spends the entire fifth day creating the animals that inhabit the sky and the sea: fowl and fish, among others. On the sixth day, God turns his attention to the animals of the earth, cattle and creeping things and wild animals of every kind—oh, and also, human beings, whom God creates in God's image. It can be humbling or elevating knowing *all* of us mammals are just one day's work. After all that labor, on the seventh day, God kicks back and has a beer.

In the second creation story, the order of creation is reversed. First, God makes the human male, then plants a garden in Eden to give the man something to beautify his world and occupy his time. Realizing that the man needs a partner to share in such paradise, God creates the animals to be Adam's companions. God accomplishes all of this as if hoping for a significant partnership between the human and the animal realms. As it turns out, only Eve can supply the kind of mutuality and interdependence that Adam sought. Still, the story emphasizes the significance of the animal world in God's plan and purpose for all creation.

In my own life, I have often glimpsed such God-given ambition from our animal friends. Thus, many of these stories reveal what I've learned from all manner and sort of living things: tree-topping frogs, seafaring stingrays, rodeo hogs, desert critters, and sacrificial sand dollars. Interwoven into the tapestry of life itself, these creatures can teach us a great deal about love, faith, hope, joy, spirituality, and living—about all that is essential in this life. In particular, my own dog Sam has been a source of significant inspiration for many years. The stories in this book have been written and compiled over the course of Sam's life and the seasons of our shared existence. I am grateful for our God-given partnership that has allowed us to evolve, explore, change, develop, and mature together. Sharing life with Sam has not only helped me survive the challenges of human existence, it has taken me closer to Eden than I ever imagined possible.

I did not initially set out to write about animals and faith. They just kept nuzzling their way into the narrative, in the same way that Sam sticks his nose between me and my newspaper and refuses to move until he has received the attention due him. As it turns out, these blessed beasts make for some good storytelling. In their supporting, incidental, and metaphorical roles, they make us aware of a world bigger and broader than our narrow agendas and exclusive insights.

A favorite liturgical moment in my life as a parish priest is the Annual Blessing of the Pets associated with the Feast Day of St. Francis. I am consistently amazed at the profound level of love that links all God's creatures gathered on that day. The service is chaotic, unpredictable, touching, and full of grace, so symbolic of the spiritual life God calls us to live. When a human being stands before me and names his or her pet, I am reminded of that second creation story in which God brings all the animals to Adam and allows Adam to name them. It is an intimate moment we share and a privileged position I bear—to reach out, touch, and pronounce God's blessing on one of God's great blessings.

Admittedly, I am no modern-day Saint Francis. My family and my exes will tell you that "Saint" belongs nowhere near my name, and I'd rather you not call me "Francis" anyway. You see, I still prefer some of my animals filleted and grilled, others lightly breaded and deep-fried. If I am going to tell the story, I must tell the whole story—a story not limited to the sentimental context of stuffed teddy bears and cuddly cartoon characters. No, here follow the dog bites, the bee stings, the slaughterhouse, the fires, the fakes, the fur—for if God hallows any of life, God must hallow all of it. Truth is large, and God is big enough to handle it.

In a real sense, this book parallels my own spiritual journey. I've come a long way from that day in third grade when Chris Enoch's dachshund chased me from his backyard, taking a significant portion of my left calf as I fled. Today, I trust my dog Sam and his big teeth to be wedged tightly among my most private parts. My fundamentalist upbringing taught me to fear God and to run from the world. I have since learned to trust God and to embrace the world. Religious acts are no longer performed out of a guilt-ridden sense of duty, but out of a passion-driven sense of joy. And I have become keenly aware that the true test of faith is not "What do you believe?" but rather, "Can I trust you?" Real, authentic religion is trustworthy above all else.

Such a posture of familiarity does not begin to deplete my reservoir of reverence. I still stand in awe of the world around me. Nor do I assume an exhaustive knowledge of God, life, or anything for that matter. The spiritual path is unpredictable, contradictory, and changing; and I am constantly aware that a new adventure, lesson, or insight is just around the next corner, always a mere dogleg away.

Once, the story goes, Moses moseyed up a mountain in the middle of nowhere to see some scrub brush that had inexplicably caught fire. From that flaming shrub, Moses heard the voice of God say, "Take off your shoes; you're standing on holy ground." He did, and he never saw things the same way again. I'm sure it was quite a stretch for Moses then, as it is a stretch for us now, until we remember that holy ground is often found in the most unlikely of places.

So kick off your shoes. Read on. The ground we share is holy indeed.

PART ONE

••••••••••

Puppy Breath

•

CHAPTER 1

············

The Gospel According to Sam

It is hard on the ego to acknowledge that my dog is more famous than I will ever be. Sam's popularity is mostly the product of his naïve and selfless love toward all living creatures—dogs, cats, humans, lizards, and bugs. Sam has a genuine interest in you, no matter who you are. He wants to love you. He wants to lick you. By comparison, I am reasonably popular, but much more selective. Sam is Jesus. I am Paul. And I limit whom I lick.

Much of Sam's notoriety can be attributed to the Great Mother's Day Fire of 1995. At 11:38 a.m., on Sunday, May 14, my ex-girlfriend Rachel was putting in a rare appearance at my parish, St. James Episcopal in Austin, when a gas leak triggered an explosion at her apartment. (See why you should always be in church?) Sam was caught in the fiery fray.

As the wave of flame swept toward Sam, he ran and hid in a closet. Thank God Rachel was a less than meticulous housekeeper, so Sam had plenty to burrow under.

Now just when you think the world is going to hell in a handbasket, and that everyone has joined the militia movement or behaves like a better-dealing NFL owner, along come some good people willing to risk their own well-being and do something heroic, even for a nonhuman. Hope springs eternal.

Instead of running away from the danger, the two guys next door, Cliff and Dan, grabbed a garden hose and raced up the rickety, old wooden stairs. Seeing the flames through the shattered windows dance defiantly around the room and hearing Sam's pathetic whimpering from his makeshift shelter, Cliff kicked in the door and started dousing the fire. Another neighbor, Dick, rushed in after them, found Sam peeking out from a pile of panties, and carried him to safety.

Sam was scorched (no hot dog jokes, please), but the neighbors were prepared. Scott, across the alleyway, phoned the vet's office to tell them Sam Houston had been burned and was on his way, while Dale pulled his car around and played paramedic. He picked up Sam and whisked him to the vet's office faster than you can implement a hint from Heloise (such as how to get seared, soggy, doggy hair off auto upholstery).

When the fire department arrived minutes later, Sam was in an ICU, and all the major network affiliates were interviewing onlookers for the 5 o'clock news. Apparently, it had been a slow news day. The neighbors had even choreographed their response for Rachel's arrival. They had thought of everything.

While our hearts were warmed, Sam appeared severely burned. The newspaper said he was "singed"—never believe what you read in the newspaper. To add insult to injury, the fire inspector accused Sam of starting the fire. Now Sam is very intelligent and can do a trick or two, but turning on the gas jet is not one of them! Still, the fire inspector's official report effectively labeled Sam an arsonist.

In addition to being on television that night, Sam appeared on the front page of the paper the next morning, wet and hairless. His stylist was not amused. The first line of the article read, "Sam Houston is one lucky dog." As I read that report out loud to Sam several days later, he looked up at me with his bloated body, almost-blinded eyes, a pink nub that used to be a nose, the remnants of a mouth, crispy critter ears, barbecued butt, scorched underbelly, roasted weenie, swollen legs, and head drooping all the way to the ground, as if to ask, "*This* is lucky?" As I said, don't believe everything you read.

A week later the neighbors threw Sam a big get-well party and proclaimed him the mayor of Baylor Street. There were large banners unfurled: "Get Well Sam!" and "Sam Is Innocent!" All of Sam's friends were there. All kinds, colors, sexes, orientations, and most species—a little anticipation of the afterlife. There was homemade ice cream to soothe his seared schnozz, and his tail wagged until it bled on the porch.

For a while, Sam couldn't lie down without enduring excruciating pain. He remained standing a lot those first few days. He would look at me questioningly, wondering how the hell he was supposed to get comfortable and why it hurt so badly. He even tried to smile on occasion. But the tail wagged on, even when it hurt.

Despite our best efforts, Sam's ears never healed, and after a few weeks they had to be amputated. He wore a blue and white wrap around his head which looked like a habit while what was left of his ears recuperated. We called him Mother Teresa. He was not amused. Rachel asked the vet whether Sam would ever be cute again after the ear surgery—which, as an Airedale pup, he most certainly had been. In his most pastoral bedside manner, the vet told us, "God, no!"

When the habit-wrap started to come off and exposed a portion of Sam's eerie-looking ear, neither of us would get near it. In fact, we both ran in opposite directions, screaming with fear at the sight of those alien appendages. For months, Sam looked like a space-invading wombat from another planet. In a B-movie. With bad makeup. And cheap costumes. Not exactly cauliflower ears, but every bit as ugly. More like rutabagas or shriveled, pink prune slices. If a Cabbage Patch Kid wrestled professionally for about fifty years, he'd end up with those ears. The vet was right. Sam was downright ugly. We wondered if there were any convents where we could cloister an ugly dog, but Mother Teresa had her hands full.

Sam got better, thanks to twelve hundred dollars worth of vet visits, a few exams at the dog ophthalmologist (talk about specialization!), three different kinds of eye drops, assorted antibiotic tablets, aspirin, and a freezer full of popsicles. Oh, and some neighbors who cared and had dared to save his life. The day the black spot appeared on his nose, we called our parents and took pictures. Soon, the spot began to spread until his nose was black again, and hair finally grew around his ears.

Although I'd love him if he looked like a leprous weasel, Sam is now cuter than ever. It's just that instead of looking like an adorable Airedale, he now resembles a big teddy bear. He has also been called a bowl of oatmeal, a shaggy carpet, and Ramen noodles with a perm. Call him what you will: I'm just glad he's well. E.T. ears and all.

Sam's rescue, reception, and recovery reminded me that although the kingdom's consummation has not happened yet, and the ultimate good life looms just beyond the horizon, we occasionally get a glimpse of the goods, a foretaste of heaven in the here and now. Saint Augustine used to call the bread and wine of the Holy Eucharist "the hors d'oeuvres of God." It's good and satisfying, but it's just an appetizer compared with the future feast. In the meantime, life can be a bitch. We endure loss, pain, and gas explosions. The Cubs are not in the World Series. And we all get burned. Without an occasional popsicle and tender pat, we'd all tuck our tails and die.

Just before his ascension, Jesus promised the disciples that he would not leave them alone. Interestingly, the One he promised to send was called the Advocate or the Comforter. The Greek word used for the Spirit is *paracletos*, which literally means, "one called alongside to help." It evokes images of daring neighbors who come to your rescue even at their own risk. Spirit-filled people are the ones who run toward you when all hell breaks loose, your life falls apart, your apartment explodes, and your dog gets a bad case of the uglies. The ones who run in the opposite direction are full of something else.

Once I participated in a funeral in which the preacher spoke of life on this earth as a constant engagement with the storm. Wherever we find ourselves, we are either in a storm, heading toward a storm, or have just gotten out of a storm. While we cannot change the weather, we can choose where we take shelter. We cannot control our circumstances, but we can choose where to live. We can also get to know our neighbors and decide to be neighbors in return.

Not long after Sam's ordeal, an intelligent, well-meaning man wrote a newspaper column about informing his son that the family dog would not join them in heaven, for the dog had no soul. Apparently, the man had thought he'd read such nonsense in the Bible and that he was doing his son a great service by setting the record straight. Well, I've never met that man's dog, and I do not doubt his sincerity. I do know I have learned a lot about the soul from Sam. About suffering and significance. About living and licking. About wagging and wisdom. About vulnerability. Giving. Tolerance. Sacrifice. Community. Compassion. About loving your neighbor as you love yourself.

Now I could be barking up the wrong tree, but it seems to me that there's some small bone of soul buried beneath those paw prints. Profound ground, made holy by the shared gift. For all of these, as I read them, are signs of the spirit. Keys to the kingdom. Hallmarks of heaven. The Gospel. According to Sam.

CHAPTER 2

....

Stingrays and Stereotypes

"I've planned an afternoon excursion for the whole family," my brother informed us. "We're taking a sailboat out to swim with stingrays."

"Did you say stingrays?" I inquired. "Those menacing evil sea monsters born in the bowels of hell? Those scary satanic saucers with nuclear warheads protruding from their behinds? Those flailing, violent aqua nightmares, who impersonate flounders and live solely to sever one of my limbs?"

"Relax," my brother said. "They're tame."

Where is Flipper when you need him? I wondered. I would rather take my chances with Shamu in a Jacuzzi. I'd rather perform dental hygiene on Jaws. Well, actually, I'd rather just hang out at the pool with the Hawaiian Tropic girls. But no! Here we are in Paradise, and we're hitching a ride to Hades!

My only prior experience with a stingray had been as an impressionable child. Someone accidentally landed one on a rod and reel in the murky Gulf of Mexico during the eerie predawn hours on a fishing pier populated by the cast of *Night of the Living Dead*. Not a happy meal, that catch! I swore then and there I would never surf again without a full suit of armor.

"Are you sure you wouldn't want to sip rum punch at the swim-up bar instead?" I implored.

It was too late. The trip was already paid for, and I did not want to look like the lone wuss in a family of fourth-generation Texans.

The afternoon sailing excursion to Grand Cayman's Stingray Sandbar was pleasant enough. A little sunbathing up top on my Big Dog towel had bolstered my bravado. The warm tropical breeze and ever-changing hues of blue had lowered my heart rate. A quick detour to dive for a conch shell had reinforced my resolve. But when we drew near to our ultimate destination, my heart sank faster than the anchor as monstrous gray masses, armed atomic submarines, submerged destroyers with laser tails, surrounded us and demanded our stash of conch. I had no choice but to dive in. As I put mask to water, I expected to come face-to-face with one of Beelzebub's offspring. Instead, I gazed into the eyes of the smiley-face prototype, the underwater version. He winked and rubbed his belly on my face.

I was wrong about stingrays. They are soft as velvet (okay, velvet with a thin layer of Mr. Slime) and polite as Miss Manners (well, a really hungry Miss Manners with PMS, perhaps). Their skin is smoother than a young woman's legs (that is, if she's European). For a few moments I was in Caribbean Candyland as inside-out moon pies brushed by and Oreos minus-an-outside-cookie darted between my legs. The stingray stereotypes simply didn't hold water. The Hawaiian Tropic girls could have the afternoon off.

On Ninth Street in Austin, between Baylor and Blanco, lives an Airedale named Bexar who epitomizes refinement in the canine realm. He even manages to squat, or rather to lower his loins gracefully, in a majestic manner. Upon passing by, I would not be at all startled to see Bexar smoking a pipe, reading a book, or preparing for a lecture. I believe he'd be an authority on Oscar Wilde. It was Bexar who first turned Rachel and me on to Airedales, which later led to our adoption of Sam Houston.

Upon meeting Bexar, I immediately went to the bookstore and bought a book on Airedales. The most common description of said breed was that Airedales are consistently "dignified and aloof." There was no living creature more dignified and aloof than the stately, distinguished Bexar. Even when he hid a tennis ball in the recesses of his throat and regurgitated it up on the grass, he did so with great aplomb. How we longed for our new "dignified and aloof" dog, a dog so composed he would not even shed. And then we got Sam.

Oh, yeah, Sam is dignified and aloof all right. Just like Jim Carrey or Jerry Lewis. And Shaquille O'Neal is petite and Lyle Lovett has a flat top. Sam is Gomer Pyle with fur. Larry, Curly, and Moe with a dog collar. He is the alien love child of Erkel and Roseanne, trained at the Dennis Rodman School of Etiquette. Too bad Sam didn't have an agent during *The Dukes of Hazzard* or *The Beverly Hillbillies*. He'd have made me a fortune. He's the thickest of the thick, the hickest of the hick, as refined as the Texas sweet crude under the Greenpeace headquarters. He is part sloth, part fanny pack. He has an obsession with crotches even Freud could not cure. He is an eighty-two-pound lapdog even when there is no lap. He produces enough drool and slobber to make a dent in a West Texas drought.

Sam is not dignified or aloof—and he sheds everywhere. So much for Airedale stereotypes. The only personality trait that Sam and Bexar share is that they both pee on trees.

For many years, I was a priest at a predominantly African American Episcopal church on Austin's East Side. Early in my tenure, our building was falling apart, leaking like a sieve. One day a nice white lady from a nice white church with lots of money from Austin's West Side came over to check out our facility. We were hoping she'd write a nice check of any color. When I showed her the nursery, whose ceiling happened to have washed away in the last flood, she pointed out the angels upon the wall. These particular angels were your basic cutesy cherub-type angels, the ones that do well with babies. She pointed to the cutesy black angel on the wall, looked at me, and gave me a cutesy angel giggle.

Generally, I am not perturbed by cutesy angel giggles, but this one bugged the hell out of me. It was quite obvious that, to this nice white lady, this black angel was especially cutesy, even absurd, because of his ethnicity. We all know, she implied with her cutesy and not altogether ill-meaning glance, that angels are white. How absolutely precious and utterly adorable to paint one black!

I once told this story to a group of fine, young fraternity boys at an outstanding university. Those boys were just as nice as nice could be. They'll grow up to coach Little League and vote for respectable candidates. They'll all invest in the stock market. Some may cheat on their wives, but few will be arrested for possession of a controlled substance. When I described the angels on the nursery wall as being black, several of them laughed out loud. Not an evil laugh, mind you, not at all. No, it was a good white-boy laugh, almost cutesy but a little too obnoxious. A hearty, certainly innocent chuckle at the thought of a black angel.

For we all know that angels are white, stingrays are mean, and Airedales are dignified and aloof. Cutesy giggles and innocent laughs can destroy a civilization. And that's not funny. Stereotypes tell us of nothing more than our own ignorance; but maybe someday we'll dive a little deeper, and come face-to-face with the truth.

CHAPTER 3

....

Dog Spelled Backwards

No fan of formulae, I am not much into catechizing, creedalizing, or categorizing. For me, systematic theology is a long-winded oxymoron. However, a small portion of an African catechism provides perhaps the best explanation I have ever read as to why we exist:

Question: Why did God make you?
Answer: Well, God thought you just might like it!

God thought we just might like it. And most of us, more often than not, do. As good a reason as any to be created.

There are many dogs in my neighborhood. There's Georgie, the pathologically active Schnauzer (you may add the prefix "hyper" to the adjective of your choice). Gatsby, her laid-back brother with the derriere so distinctively defined I'd swear he has silicone buttock implants. Gus, the sweet-natured golden Lab. Rusty, the neighborhood tough who roams freely in silver-studded collar sans leash. Bear, a pure-bred blubbering beast of unknown breed. Bitsy, the buck-toothed cutie who runs the world from the window of her one-bedroom apartment. Of all of these there is only one who is mine. Only one who is allowed to ruin my life and retain my love, and all because I thought we both might like it.

When Rachel and I broke up years ago, neither of us was willing to part with our only child, even if he is a nonhuman, so we decided upon joint custody. I never fail to pay dog support. During many a visit, Sam has been a pain in my behind until I removed my wallet and handed over all my money to the veterinarian. I have spent most of my inheritance to possess the great knowledge that Sam has dry skin. Antibiotics. Antihistamines. Alpha Keri. It all adds up. So, after dropping a bundle on a particular visit at the vet's office to hear once again how dry skin is common to the breed, I left Sam at home while I went to the bank to take out a second mortgage, then to the pawn shop to see what I could get for the unchewed furniture.

I live fairly simply and don't have many valuable possessions. My ex-wife took the Doonesbury original, so I'm down to a small collection of priceless ancient antiquities: a Hellenistic oil lamp, a Roman plate, a Bronze Age cup, and the most beautiful and valuable, a lovely juglet from the Iron Age, simply yet exquisitely crafted, in perfect condition. The archaeologist (grave robber) I purchased them from in Jerusalem was most reluctant to part with the juglet. This timeless piece had survived war, drought, famine, occupation, revolution, the birth of a couple of world religions, and cultural chaos for several millennia. Ironically, it could not survive a few hours of Sam.

When I got home that day, Sam had knocked the three-thousand-year-old juglet off the shelf and onto the floor and had broken off a large chunk of its elegant neck. I stood there, stunned. I had several options. Sam steaks. A sadistic spanking. An S.P.C.A.–sanctioned safari. Instead, I just forgave him. He may be one blankety-blank dog, but he is my blankety-blank dog and that makes all the difference.

I had dinner with a friend not long ago who, after graciously receiving some constructive criticism from my lips, told me, "You know, if there is just one person in this world who will put his arms around you and be there for you no matter what, you can put up with all the bullshit the world has to offer." So true. Add to that dog doo and human poo. And God goo, if there is such a thing.

For despite the fact that all of us are a lot more trouble than we're worth—we smell bad, we break things, we make a mess, we cost a lot, we misbehave—somebody still took a chance and brought us into the world.

So put on your boots. Grab your pooper scooper. And take your chances. Who knows? You just might like it.

CHAPTER 4

....

Forbidden Pigs

I collected pigs long before pig collecting was cool. It began innocently enough: girlfriends consistently gave me pigs as gifts (a mere coincidence, I'm sure). Before long, I was so enamored of the little porkers, I began to request them on significant gift-giving occasions. My soft spot for swine has grown into a museum-quality collection.

One afternoon while drinking margaritas by Lake Travis, I made the mistake of telling Jack and Becky Fles of my hog fetish and how I thought real pigs would make great pets. I subsequently forgot about this conversation until several months later when I received a phone call early one Saturday morning at my lovely church-owned rectory in Houston's posh Briargrove neighborhood. It was a close-in, established, Stepford suburb, not upscale enough to allow for eccentricity, but affluent enough to demand conformity. I was contemplating whether to take a quarter or a half-inch off my meticulously manicured lawn when the phone rang. The voice on the other end said she had a delivery from the Arboretum and needed directions to my home. It sounded suspiciously like Becky, and I braced myself for some unpredictable container of chaos.

She couldn't help herself, living with Jack, former director of youth ministries at St. John's Cathedral in Denver, known for his cannon ministry. Jack was fond of teaching his impressionable youth how to turn antique milk pails into powerful cannons capable of firing volleyballs into neighboring counties (much to the cathedral dean's delight). You never really knew what Jack might be up to. Sure enough, about thirty minutes later, Jack, Becky, and their daughter Keegan showed up at my front door bearing a very special gift.

This thoughtful present, so appropriate for a Briargrove backyard, was a brand-new, black and white, curly-tailed, live baby pig. Whereas my wife (now my ex-wife) was not amused, I took an instant liking to my new pet, and, given the paradoxical situation in which he found himself, I named him Kosher.

Kosher was a very motivated, talented young pig and immediately began landscaping the backyard. He dug a lovely moat around the house, transplanted all of the azaleas, and finally turned his attention to an old fence that obviously needed to be removed. Fearing that he might jog over to George and Barbara Bush's place later on, and not wanting to explain the situation to the Secret Service or my bishop, I went to the pet store to purchase a leash and other pig supplies. The closest I could come were dog and cat supplies, so I bought some of each, including a doggie brush for those special grooming occasions and a kitty litter box, thinking I would train him to use it, foolish city boy that I am.

He ran the other direction when I called "Here, Kosher," so I leashed him to a post on the back porch to make sure he wouldn't run over and introduce himself to the neighbors. He did not care for such down-home detainment, and after flailing around for an hour like bacon on a hot skillet, he resignedly pressed his baby pig cheek to the patio pavement, thrust his little pig posterior into the air, and began to cry in soft, heart-wrenching whimpers so precious they made Babe sound like a gang member.

It was perhaps the saddest scene I have ever encountered. It was enough to turn George Foreman into a vegetarian. The neighbor's children then started to scream at the top of their lungs, "Look, Mommy, that priest has a piggy in his yard."

Briargrove was probably no place for a pig. So, for the remainder of his life on this earth, Kosher lived on a farm in Baytown, although I'm not sure that's where he belonged either. For there he simply grew fat, and probably ended up on someone's barbecue grill (maybe right back in a Briargrove backyard).

I sometimes wonder about where he truly belonged, if he ever really had a home, if he ever found his element, and why I never even got a slab of bacon out of the deal. Hey, that kitty litter was expensive! I have wondered if, after the divorce, maybe Kosher and I and the Briargrove Homeowner's Association couldn't have worked things out. I still wonder, though not very often.

I got somewhat emotional over Kosher several years later while attending the swine auction at the Houston Livestock Show and Rodeo. It's not often that I get to wear boots and bolo. My good friend Michael Soper served on the swine committee that year. It's quite an honor, they say, much more prestigious than the poultry committee, for example. Visions of sugar plum swinies danced in my head as I headed whole hog toward the Dome. I paid my three-dollar parking fee and walked right through the midway, untempted, past the Ferris wheel and the Kamikaze, the cotton candy and the yard-long hot dogs. I paid another four bucks to enter the Astrohall and take in the rich aroma of rank, rural residue. Give me a city sewer any day.

I wandered through the Astromaze in search of my beloved porkers, past the Tamale Barn, Sassy Sam's, Marcia's Crystal Earth, and the Instant Heat Booth (a real hot seller in Houston, I'm sure). Still, no sight of swine. I boot-scooted my way clear across the hall, sidestepping longhorn land mines, and around the monster truck exhibit. I two-stepped toward the Astroarena as booths became blurred—E & B Trailer Sales, Caricatures by Katy, Unique Baskets, etc.—I had no time for any of them. Finally, just beyond the Thick Foam Genuine Imitation Cowhide Padded Snap-On Seat Covers and across from the Bing Crosby Indian Art, I heard an auctioneer call the hogs over the sooey shouts of pig purchasers.

"Are you a buyer?" asked the burly, bearded cowboy guarding the door.

I hesitated. Knowing I had about thirty bucks in my back pocket, just enough to buy a pig snout or perhaps just a nose hair, I said, "Yup," and hustled by, into a sea of gimme caps, wide brims, tight jeans, and rhinestone studs. Gold-jacketed waiters served trough-sized cocktails to duded-up cowboys with stuffed red razorbacks peering over their hats. Decked-out cowgirls flashed pink bandanas that read, "The days of swine and roses." There were trophies, bouquets, fancy 4-H banners, lots of big hair and broad shoulders. But where, oh where, were the pigs?

Finally, I saw her off in a corner: the biggest behemoth I ever laid eyes on, a cream-colored lass as large as Lithuania, a sedan-sized sow totally uninterested in all the fuss, choosing to smell, and later eat, the rose wreath around her neck. "That's one purdy pig," I briefly considered hollering. The auctioneer might have misinterpreted my gesture and with my luck I'd unload my entire life's savings on two tons of pork butt, the highest-priced ham this side of heaven. Nope. I decided to sit there and pretend to be a cowboy and a buyer. I fooled no one in such a setting.

So after I became bored with both boars and boors I moseyed on outta there, and returned to my previous city-slickin' ways. I guess I'm just an urban cowboy, anyway. Yes sir. Me and John Travolta.

When I lived in Chicago, I had two basic choices when it came to hearing the blues. I could head up north, home of the trendier-than-thou and listen to some mighty fine blues with a bunch of people who looked just like me, only better. Or I could stay down on the south side and sneak over to the Checkerboard Lounge and hear some "damn right I've got the blues" blues. It was downhome blues with an edge: a chilly, soft-smokin' steel-eyed edge that made you feel like that night's blue light special, just paranoid enough to sneak frequent over-the-shoulder peeks and squirm in your slum-school reject seat.

I would often integrate the place when I walked in, and although never made to feel unwelcome, I was never invited to move in either. Buddy Guy, one of the great blues guitarists of all time, had recently purchased the Checkerboard Lounge, and on my first visit he performed a blues anthology that would have made Muddy proud. Toward the end of his two-hour tribute, he explained why he performed at this dilapidated dive instead of those stylish clubs sheltered by skyscraper shadows. He said simply, "You can't take a ham hock and cook it downtown." Not bad advice for any seeker.

You can't take a ham hock and cook it downtown. You can't turn a backyard into a barnyard in Briargrove. You can't purchase a sow's ear with a silk purse full of money. You can't franchise authenticity. You can't get the good stuff home-delivered. You can't buy anything soulful on sale. Any serious search may not be close and may not be cheap, but I refuse to settle for Memorex and museums. If it isn't live, it isn't life.

So, the collection continues to grow. Porky. Pinky. Wilbur. Old Major. Arnold. Piglet. Pigasaurus. Miss Piggy. Ralph the Swimming Pig. The Yorkshire Hog. Piggy Bank. Pork Chop.

I am still not sure where God lives, but I am quite certain God gets around. I am still not sure precisely where I belong, but the more I journey, the better I get at narrowing it down.

So, the itinerary broadens. The cathedral in the city. The little country church. The seminary. The sanctuary. The monastery. The cemetery. The confessional. The whorehouse. The outhouse. The mosque. The temple. The pulpit. The pub. The mountain. The valley. The sea. The wide open spaces. The backyard. The rodeo. The southside. The here. The now. The known. The unknown.

And the search goes on.

Others will want to follow you. Don't get hog-tied. No piggy-backs allowed. Remember the words of Jesus: "Do not cast your pearls before swine." Teach them to dive. And find their own pearls. Deep down. Far away. Downtown.

CHAPTER 5

· · · · · · · · · · · ·

Chicken of the Sea

For the love of lobster. For the love of God.

My intent was definitely focused on the former as I listened to my buddy, Jack Fles, wax poetic, although hardly prophetic, about our upcoming summer sail in Maine. Through past experience I knew that any time spent with Jack typically yielded an unpredictable adventure, but his travel-guide eloquence laid an effective trap for me.

"August is the best time of year up here," he proclaimed. Jack painted a picture-perfect postcard of our journey. Sailing serenely through calm waters under still, blue skies. Mooring at a charming island sanctuary where we could camp placidly under the stars, bathing in the brilliant sun and becoming bronze gods. But it was the "lobster in every pot" portion of his politicking that hooked me. I bought my airline ticket faster than I could boil water.

A few weeks later, my aerodream of big, tender lobsters swimming in a sea of drawn butter was cut short by an abrupt landing in Boston and the sudden realization of a recently suppressed truth. *It's always an adventure with the Fles family*, I reminded myself as the plane approached the gate.

Jack and Becky Fles were to pick me up at the airport and drive me to their home in Gardiner, Maine. Early the next day, we would depart from scenic Rockland Harbor on their annual Christ Church sailing trip, aptly named the Christ Church Sailing Adventure: five vessels and thirty-two passengers disguised as crew members led by Captain Jack, their parish priest. I was to present each evening's reflection as we gathered around a campfire on Warren Island. I should have known, based on my experiences with previous Fles family adventures, that the evening's devotions would be the least of my worries.

I was not particularly surprised to hear, as my plane deboarded, "Paging passenger William Miller. You have an urgent message." I was actually relieved to find that my friends were simply running a little late due to traffic. Three hours later, Jack and Becky arrived.

The simple trek back to their house was a circuitous surprise. It took us the better part of the day to get out of Boston. Our first stop was at Jack's doctor's office for an appointment he had conveniently forgotten to mention. We were delayed for another hour and a half as we waited for Jack's insurance company to give formal permission to proceed. Then, we ventured into the Boston suburbs to pick up Paul, a fifteen-year-old family friend, whom his mother hoped we'd "rehabilitate" on our nautical journey. Finally we crossed the state line into Maine, and immediately got lost looking for the L.L. Bean Factory Outlet. Jack was out of clean socks, so he figured, why not just stop and buy some new ones instead? After coming within two fumes of running out of gas on the outskirts of Gardiner, itself on the outskirts of nowhere, we finally coasted into the parsonage at midnight.

The next morning we were up at five and on the road to Rockland by six. Jack and I with our car full of young men made a detour to the local IGA supermarket because, as Jack said proudly, "You've got to try their BLTs." I was hoping for lobster and eggs.

It proved to be a most unfortunate breakfast choice, since Jack had left with Becky's van keys. The van held all of our food, luggage, Jack's family members, and three other sailors who were eager to get to Rockland. Realizing what had happened, Becky jumped on her bicycle and pedaled furiously after us, screaming all the way through town, ungodly behavior for an ungodly hour. The new Episcopal priest and his family were already making quite an impression in town. She lost us just after we made the turn for the BLTs.

We proceeded to miss our cutoff to Rockland ("Mainers don't use maps," Jack retorted) and lost the poor teenaged driver who was attempting to follow us ("He should've been paying attention," Father Fles intoned).

Three hours later, we all somehow managed to depart Rockland Harbor in our respective vessels.

My first assigned task as a sailor was to secure the bumpers to the boat. The procedure was simple enough, Jack instructed: (1) tie the bumper on, and (2) toss it over the side of the boat. But I got the order reversed—Popeye, I'm not. And Jack used language unbecoming of the priesthood. After a series of retrieval events that could not have been choreographed better by the Three Stooges, we secured our bumpers and puttered out of the harbor. Finally, on the beautiful open waters of Penobscot Bay, on a gloriously sunny day, we turned off our engines, hoisted our sails, and the wind immediately died. A few hours later our engine followed.

"There's a town just over yonder where we can get help and buy fresh lobsters for the evening meal," Jack assured us. *Yonder*—a theological term meaning "we pray that it exists." After an afternoon of endless drifting, occasional sailing, and fervent praying, we arrived at yonder, and there was a town, Lincolnville.

Coming in, we missed the mooring ball enough times to retire the side had we been a baseball team, but finally secured the vessel in the harbor. Our applause and shouts of joy were cut short by a simple "Uh-oh." We all looked sternward and saw that the dinghy, the small boat which we would row to shore, had come untied and was quickly drifting out to sea. Keegan, Jack's seven-year-old daughter, observed, "The last time this happened, we were stuck for three days." No one laughed, for we all knew that Keegan probably spoke the truth.

After another unplanned sail out of the harbor in pursuit of the lost dinghy, we secured it again. We coaxed a mechanic onboard, who diagnosed our engine's ills as "You're out of gas." This should not have been a problem. All harbor towns in Maine sell gas and lobsters. All, that is, except one—Lincolnville. No gas, no lobsters. My theology of yonder was only too true. Late that night, we were rescued by a park ranger, a brawny, lobster-tossin', moose-wrestlin' Mainer woman who whisked us across the bay at warp speed, daring lobster pots to tangle in her propeller.

Beyond midnight we arrived at Warren Island, and, let's just say, I now clearly understand the concept of primitive camping—and never want to do it again. As I pressed my frigid face to the damp plastic tarp which was my bed, though miserable in my surroundings, I was comforted by my single-focused dream. Grilled lobster. Baked lobster. Sautéed lobster. Lobster stew. Lobster tacos. Lobster salad. Lobster burgers. Lobster casserole. Lobster bisque. Lobster tail. Lobster claw. Lobster whatever else is edible on a lobster. Surely that postcard Jack had described would finally come to pass the next morning, and all of our efforts would not have been in vain.

I was wrong. Again.

The next day we returned to Lincolnville only to discover that the dinghy was, once more, missing in action. After a frantic search, we found it onshore resting safely in a stall near the dock. We picked it up and immediately dropped it on Jack's foot and broke his toe. Finally, rowing our way back to the sailboat, we were met by an angry lobsterman who zipped out of nowhere in a mean little skiff powered by a smoke-belching motor. He began to circle us like a shark. Finally he approached, leered at us over his weathered scowl and growled, "It's mine, the law of the sea says it is. You stole it back." After successfully intimidating our faint-hearted crew, the pirate pulled away empty-handed, leaving us in a chilly wake of fish heads and lobster dregs. At least we had our dinghy—attached and intact. Whew! And I thought Texas cowboys were tough.

We put the sail on upside down, got fogged in the next day and rained on another. When we did get back to the Fles's house in Gardiner, tired, filthy, and smelling of four days of salt and sea, we discovered that Jack and Becky had forgotten their house keys and we were locked out. Paul, the juvenile-delinquent-in-training, keenly observed, "Like Bill says, it's always an adventure with the Fles family."

Oh, there is one small addendum to the adventure. One of the sailboats was a beautiful old rental, and it had to be sailed about four hours up the coast the next morning to its berth. After the sailing fiasco, I relished my newly discovered identity as a landlubber first-class and longed to keep my feet firmly planted on dry land, but out of loyalty to Jack, I volunteered to work the crew. The next morning, however, Jack decided that I had suffered enough, had pity on me, and let me sleep in.

Several hours later, I was wide awake and wondering what had happened when Becky returned from dropping him off in Rockland. She held out a bag of lobsters in a preemptive effort to ease my forthcoming pain. Attempting to divert my attention to the five-pound consolation prizes, she waved my big crustacean buddies in my face.

"You're not going to believe what I just witnessed," she confided in the tone of voice of someone who had just thrown away your winning lottery ticket. "There were four beautiful young women from New York—two models, a cameraperson, and a film director waiting on the dock. They asked Jack if they could film a music video on the boat as he sailed them up the coast."

Then I used language unbecoming of the priesthood. Language I had learned from Jack.

When Jack arrived home later that evening, he was smoking a cigarette and wearing a very wide grin on his very wide face. Before he could boast of God's providence, I quickly pointed out that I had spent the day in prayer and meditation. Therefore, in the spiritual sea, he was most certainly a minnow to my whale.

"So, Beck told you about our crew members, did she?" he asked, with a less than saintly glimmer in his eye.

I said to him simply, "Jack, not only are you no longer my friend, but I am convinced as of this day that *there is no God!*"

I was kidding. Mostly.

For, mostly, we are conditioned to believe that the Cosmic Navigator, when charting our course, will plan an obstacle-free, "just thinking of me" itinerary. And that our Heavenly Travel Agent would never book us on anything other than a serene, sweetness-and-light afternoon excursion to personal paradise, where the piña coladas flow freely, the bartender wears a bikini, and the weather always cooperates.

My adventure in Maine and my faith in God tell me otherwise. God's call rarely comes to us by way of a stress-free vacation on a luxury liner. We are naïve, if not cowardly, to assume that on our spiritual journey we will cross the sea on a self-contained cruise ship, sustained by an all-you-can-eat seafood buffet, and supported by animal-shaped floaties as we soak in a soothing hot tub. The soft-pedaled, popular gods of stability, success, and security are ultimately as lasting as a two-week time-share, and may be antonyms of faithfulness. In the kingdom of God, we may not always get what we want or want what we need, and we may discover that lobsters are not always what they're cracked up to be.

Jonah was the first sailor to learn this law of the sea. God called Jonah to a task that was not self-serving, to go and share a message of hope with people Jonah could not stand. Jonah immediately set sail in the opposite direction. On his aquatic adventure, he discovered that the waves get choppy, the skies get cloudy, and the itinerary is most unpredictable—that is, when God is involved. After spending four days in a fish belly (some suggest a whale's, more likely a shark's), Jonah has a change of heart, repents, and God rescues him by way of having the fish regurgitate him onto a hostile beach. (Note: salvation in the form of fish puke.)

Jonah finally heeds God's call and ventures into enemy territory and does what he's supposed to do. The 120,000 inhabitants of the city of Nineveh *and* all their animals are saved. Mission accomplished, Jonah goes back to the beach and spreads a blanket under a palm tree. The bizarre story ends with God commissioning a special worm to eat the palm tree so the sun will bear down on Jonah's bald head.

It seems that the call of the Almighty is not for the faint of heart. Being too comfortable, content, or complacent is not allowed. Sure, you can choose to stay home, watch vacation videos, order chicken liver delivery, and boast of God's blessing. Or you can venture into the unknown, ride out a few storms, wage war against worms and sharks, watch the models float by just beyond reach, and have the trip of a lifetime—or an eternity. It is always an adventure in the kingdom of God.

It's a trip worth taking.

I'd do it all over again. For the love of lobster. And the love of God.

CHAPTER 6

....

Cowboys Don't Wear Purple

I used to despise the desert. I found it ugly, barren, lifeless, uninviting. I would argue for hours with my college roommate from Tucson as to whether there was any beauty or purpose at all to be found in the desert, a place where the botanical and zoological worlds conspired to keep me away. "Name one desert plant or animal that doesn't have horns, needles, scales, pinchers, stickers, stingers, spines, or fangs," I'd demand. Maybe it was those four long years in West Texas, where the rattlesnake roundup crowned its own beauty queen, where they would spray-paint the grass green, where your socks turned orange after an afternoon run, where you went swimming in drunken bean soup, where it rained dust more often than water.

I would long for that deep, damp thicket of East Texas. I would dream of wrestling grinning alligators and portly possums right down into the swamp. I would fantasize about breathing soggy air and being surrounded and forced to surrender by a battalion of fat, lazy, loblolly pines.

I used to think as I gazed upon those vast expanses of dirt, rock, and cacti, "There is *nothin'* out there that I'm interested in; in fact, there's *nothin'* out there!"

I used to avoid Lent. I found it depressing, stark, silent, and austere. Forty long days in the wilderness with all this talk about penitence and frailty. Too much introspection, somber reflection, and serious mood.

I would long for the playful revelry of Easter. I would dream of the chaotic drama of Pentecost. I would fantasize about the hopeful celebration of Christmas.

I used to think, as I gazed upon that penitential purple, that stripped-down and simplified altar, that contemplative, barebones liturgy, that downsized, confessional, faithful remnant of a congregation, "There is *nothing* out there I'm interested in; in fact, there is *nothing* out there!"

I used to think that way. That is, until I went there, all the way in. I didn't just stand on the periphery and take a few snapshots of the vista. I didn't hokey-pokey in and right back out. I actually stripped down to my skivvies, the bare essentials of my existence, and I wandered around a while in that wilderness. Walked with the tarantulas. Camped out under the desert stars. Journeyed deep into one of those majestic canyons. I tried on that penitential purple and found that it made for excellent hiking attire. I sought solitude in retreat. I looked inward, alone, for a long time. It took some getting used to, but now I am indebted to the desert.

Our lives are just too crowded. We are being strangled by living things that we have planted, fed, and watered, which now threaten our existence and overrun our spaces. Every corner, every crevice, every conceivable opening has been filled. We are surrounded by so much life that we are dying. Our souls have become the Las Vegas strip, and even a couple of billion-dollar resorts will not renew or refresh us. We need some vastness, some barrenness, some fallow ground on which we can rediscover ourselves, reawaken our souls, and re-ignite the spirit who leads us to such places. For Lent, I went back to Big Bend, this time to the Ranch, a half-million acres or so of complete nothingness. My friend David, the Latin guitarist with blonde hair, went with me.

On the way, we stopped in Alpine and had upscale western cuisine at Reata (yup, the ranch in *Giant*). We asked the waitress what there was to do out here. She replied, "Nothing, that's why I moved here." Good answer. Since Alpine was our last vestige of civilization, we moseyed on over to the Cinnabar and drank a Mexican beer. Why "The Cinnabar"? I asked our waitress. She replied, "Cuz that's what the owner named it." Good answer. Life is not so complicated after all. From Presidio, the onion capital of the world and the hottest spot in the nation more often than not, we found our way to the main gate. From there, it took an hour to drive to the bunkhouse.

We shared the bunkhouse with two unknown Mexican adolescents who seemed to wander in from the scrub and a group of teachers and students from West Texas A&M who were studying scorpions. The Bug Brains would head out each evening about midnight for their hunt. "We've found nine species of scorpions out here so far," they told us, "and the most found anywhere in the world is twelve." They were also catching "robber flies" and pinning them on particle board.

Our cook's name was Tony. The table scraps went to Miguel, the javelina, who roamed out back, and to the requisite dusty dog named Jake. (Unless there is at least one dog named Jake, it's not a real ranch.) Tony cooked cowboy style. The meals were so hearty, they stuck not just to your ribs, but to your entire upper torso and even oozed down into your boots. For dinner, Tony rustled up some "chicken frieds" (out here, there's no need to add "steak"— that would be redundant), unidentified frying objects big enough to be registered in some counties and baked potatoes the size of boxing gloves, topped with butter and sour cream. No cheese (too colorful), no bacon bits (bits are for horses), and no chives (too dang dandy).

Out there, there seemed to be two rules to live by: tell it like it is and savor what you have. Out there, "back at the ranch" means back at the ranch and what you see is exactly what you get. So it's not as explicit as the Rule of St. Benedict, not as rigorous as wandering in the Judean wilderness, not as dramatic as Jesus' cliff-hanging struggle with Satan. Still, the cowboy way makes for a good Lenten retreat. A nice piece of straw to dangle from your mouth and chew on for awhile.

We pulled on our boots, saddled up our horses, and rode off into the sunset each day. Actually they were hiking boots and they had to be laced. And we walked. And it was much earlier than evening. We wandered Fresno Canyon, explored the Solitario, and climbed up to Cinco Tinajas. We did not plant. We did not water. We did not build. We did not create. And God saw that it was good. And we rested.

From a distance the rock formations cast a watchful eye in our direction. Fierce almond warriors, coffee-colored carvings, antifertility African masks wedged together like a foreboding fence, scaring seeds, eating embryos, denouncing developer's dreams. These are the birth-control gods. Surveyors of solitude, purveyors of penitence, mercenaries of the metaphysical, mineral masses that omit the Absolution and the Alleluia. They wink only at real cowboys. All others they call to repent.

So I stared at the ground and walked away, unafraid and aware. I looked for a relic, a fragment of the true cross, a splinter from the ark, a piece of silver with Judas's fingerprints, even a skull from Pharaoh's cattle. I found nothing but rusty disconnected pipe and a botanical garden of survivors, growing just to spite us all. Of course, David found a horseshoe, perfectly rustic and charming and whole, slightly dented at the bend, making it even more flawless.

"It is against the law to remove anything from a state natural area," I reminded myself. "And David is a thief. I know he will steal it. I should turn him in."

He turned back and said, "Next one I find is yours." So, I misjudged.

Of course the next one was only half a horseshoe. I paused for a moment to ponder the half-shoed horse. I could relate. I hid both horseshoes in the bottom of my purple backpack and later displayed them on my bedroom shelf between the large rock of fool's gold from Leadville and my hand-painted tile from St. George's College in Jerusalem. "I found them in Big Bend," I now boast to friends, though such treasures still remind me of my inadequacies as an alchemist and archeologist.

On our way home we stopped at the Lajitas Outpost and bought a beer for the goats. Unfortunately we couldn't stay for that evening's concert featuring Cowboy Don and Tony Turbo. Too bad. The next night it would be the Folkadelics.

On the road toward the old ghost town of Terlingua I did the Texas Wave to passers-by (keep hand on steering wheel and raise slightly while nodding once). The only green in sight was prickly.

The sign read "This Road Maintained by the Chili Appreciation Society International."

We pulled into Terlingua and headed for La Kiva for a margarita. We sat on tree stumps. I was reminded of the bar scene from *Star Wars*. Everyone was there: Rambo, Easy Rider, the Marlboro Man, Mr. Clean, Davy Crockett, Cat Woman, Yogi Bear, C. Everett Koop. There were caldrons and bones on every ledge. The bones looked human. A dinosaur skeleton added to the ambiance. Behind the bar a sign read "U.S. Out of Texas." Willie Nelson and Frank Sinatra dueled it out on the jukebox. I snacked on El Diablo Chili and Nachos de Reyes. I saw the waitress eat one of my nachos before she brought them to the table. I did not complain to the management. She was licensed to carry a concealed weapon.

We headed across the highway for a final meal before we started home. After a day in the desert, I wanted to wash up before dinner. I found the restroom—outside. Back in Austin, you needed a Ph.D. in philosophy to decipher bathroom graffiti. Here, it was simple and direct. Above the urinal, proudly inscribed, in all its unadorned profundity: Speck Thomas. Lobo, Texas. No need for witticisms or cleverness out there. You just leave your mark and move on. I discovered there was no running water.

Why was I not surprised? Once again, I would eat with unclean hands.

CHAPTER 7

....

Sand-Dollar Salvation

At the opening session of a recent beach retreat, I immediately bonded with a guy named Mike, who shared with the group that the only reason he was there was because his wife agreed to let him bring a refrigerator-sized cooler filled with beer. I decided that after such a revelation, God was calling us to be prayer partners for the duration of the weekend. The spirit was indeed present whenever we got together.

Mike was an early riser and a beach walker, and so on Saturday morning, he was out on the beach before the sun could play peek-a-boo with the breakers. He was the first one out there, and as a result, he was able to find out about a dozen whole, perfectly preserved, unbroken, exquisitely formed sand dollars. At our first Saturday morning session, it was show-and-tell time for Mike. He was truly proud of his find.

He told us, "I've been coming to the beach for thirty years and I have never found so many sand dollars." He kept them safely stored in his room, far away from his ice chest and our prayer sessions.

Mike had big plans for his discovery. We had been asked by the retreat leader to participate in the homily on Sunday morning by sharing something we had found on the beach or in the water as a sort of object lesson. Mike could barely contain his excitement over the bold, beautiful masterpiece he was planning with his coastal treasure. He was going to dazzle us with the world's largest sand dollar sculpture, an artistic triumph that would amaze, astound, and bear witness to the wondrous works of God in our lives. It would be a true testimony to the material miracles God hath wrought for those who trust in His goodness.

So early Sunday morning, Mr. Sand Hog was back on the beach, scooping up even more symmetrically stunning dollars to add to his unparalleled collection. However, there was one slight problem. He noticed that on this early bird excursion, he was not alone. Not far behind him, quickly gaining ground, was another crack-of-dawn treasure seeker who also combed the beach in search of sand dollars. Mike was pissed. In the name of Jesus, of course. A self-righteous indignation inflated his soul like a Portuguese man-of-war.

He prayed for high tide, a landshark, an errant barge—anything to rid his private shore of the invading infidel. Anyone who might pummel this plundering pirate into sand pellets. Any way to keep that trespassing sinner at bay. Mike refused to let that selfish marauder gain any ground. Mike picked up the pace and left the stranger in a cloud of beach dust. Snatching whole dollars and stuffing them into his shorts, teasing the follower by tossing broken, ugly fragments onto the ground, he tantalized the intruder with the leftovers of worthless, dismembered dollars.

Mike's coastal crusade ended as he reached the far fishing pier, turned around, and headed back to the retreat site. God was with him, he convinced himself, as his pockets bulged with booty. He smiled smugly at the inferior straggler, and the stranger smiled back, stopping him with a soft touch.

"It looks like you're collecting sand dollars," he said. "I found a few. Would you take them?"

Mike's heart sank deeper than buried treasure. Actually it softened. With disbelief in his voice and a new insight in his soul, he told the gift-giver the whole story. And he asked him if his name, just by chance, might be Jesus. The man smiled and said that no, he wasn't Jesus, at least as best he knew. But often the best we know misses the Messiah in our midst. He gave Mike the God-given gifts, and Mike returned with a gift for the rest of our group.

His hastily rewritten homily began with unloading a stuffed sack of sand dollars. In silence, he delicately placed each in his palm and walked around the room and gave one to each of us until his priceless collection was given away. Then he brought out a paper plate filled with broken, discarded, fragmented pieces of sand dollars, none particularly lovely, and offered that up as a testimony of his own life. For they spoke deeply, he said, of all that we can accumulate, of all that we can offer back to God.

We were amazed, saved, and astounded. Dazzled, even. By sand dollars. And portions thereof.

CHAPTER 8

···········

Finger-Lickin' Good

I am reasonably certain that a stingray sucked my toe, producing an aesthetically unpleasing swollen area hanging over my nail like Homer Simpson's belly. It was the big toe on my right foot. I knew a young couple from Michigan in graduate school who claimed toe-sucking as one of life's Tantric pleasures, but I had never had my toe sucked until that Buffet-esque afternoon in the Caribbean.

A sailboat full of unsynchronized swimmers flailed around a stingray sandbar, while our guide tossed one of those big, happy moonies over his right shoulder and burped him like a baby. Somehow, the sight of a smiley-faced softy spitting up seawater calmed us down and enabled us to roam freely in their clear blue playpen. Nerf flying saucers with protruding ray guns brushed against our thighs and sucked tiny pieces of squid from our fingertips.

"There is nothing to fear," instructed our captain (Morgan, I think). "However, if your foot gets buried in the sand with a toe sticking out, a stingray may think it's a piece of squid and give you the hickey of your life."

Well, I knew that was impossible. The hickey of my life was given to me by Carla Shadle on a high school choir trip to Corpus Christi. I had no idea what she was doing until it was too late. Too bad I didn't own a clerical collar back then. Still, I tried in vain to keep my feet uncovered. And I truly pity that poor gray pancake of a ray who thought she was getting a little piece of the good stuff and was sorely disappointed to taste my big toe. Then again, maybe it wasn't so bad, if my friends from Michigan knew better.

I have noticed that often when I point to some incredible reality just beyond where we are—a squirrel doing back flips on a tree branch outside our window, an amazing rubber-tipped green satellite ball just ten feet away, a fluffy man toy who would make for an excellent tug-of-war game, a side of beef dangling from the refrigerator door—Sam simply stares at the end of my finger. Worse than that, Sam will often come right over to my finger and lick it. Sometimes he'll lick it three or four times, especially if I forgot to wash my hands after eating a bologna and jalapeño sandwich. The harder I point, the more emphatically I thrust my finger toward that greater reality, the more intently focused is Sam's tongue on my hand's appendages. A faint paste of cheddar wedged between the fingerprints, a slight sliver of pepperoni lodged in a cuticle, a lost crumb of Triscuit hiding beneath a nail—such molecular morsels seem to be enough to call forth Sam's undivided attention and most heroic effort.

Perhaps we've much to learn from such keen sensuality. True sustenance and satisfaction don't always get supersized or flung from a drive-through window with extra cheese, bacon, and a Big Gulp. We've become better at devouring than tasting, and our world (and our souls) suffer for it. I'm talking less than the "little somethings" Pooh longs for. I speak of quantum snacks. Not bites, sips, or nibbles. Just whiffs, gleanings, tiny, intimate experiences detected by unnamed taste buds, the ones not shown on tongue diagrams. The ones that perk up over subtleties, become aroused and engorged at fleeting possibilities. The ones that have photo-graphic memories of unmemorable moments. Such buds as sali-vate over long-forgotten sacraments, which savor the texture of Jesus on a cardboard disk three days later. A soul that is quenched by absorbing cheap, stale wine—wine that wouldn't be caught dead (or breathing) on any list. Wine slung by a novice, served only by the grace of God. Such understated spices for which there is no place in the rack, no measuring spoon small enough to contain them. For a pinch could destroy us. Or re-create us.

Bigger is not necessarily better. Satiation is not satisfaction. More is never enough. A megameal may be quick, easy, and cheap, but we walk away malnourished, its ultimate value about as sub-stantive as the wrapper it comes in.

There is a subtlety to the art of spirituality, a sixth sense that leaves more to the imagination than a full belly. This chef special-izes in nuances and shadows, what simmers slowly on the back burner. The Lord's Supper is barely an appetizer on an abbrevi-ated menu. Yet to ingest it is to live forever.

The real meal is worth the wait, and worth our undivided attention.

Mmmm. I can taste it now.

CHAPTER 9

....

Eating Squirrel

The same night he got up and took his two wives, his two maids, and his eleven chil-dren, and crossed the ford of the Jabbok. He took them and sent them across the stream, and likewise everything that he had. Jacob was left alone; and a man wrestled with him until daybreak. When the man saw that he did not prevail against Jacob, he struck him on the hip socket; and Jacob's hip was put out of joint as he wrestled with him. Then he said, "Let me go for the day is breaking." But Jacob said, "I will not let you go unless you bless me." So he said to him, "What is your name?" And he said, "Jacob." Then the man said, "You shall no longer be called Jacob, but Israel, for you have striven with God and with humans, and have prevailed." Then Jacob asked him, "Please, tell me your name." But he said, "Why is it that you ask my name?" And there he blessed him.

GENESIS 32:22–29

My father was born in Ridge, Texas. In case you are unfamiliar with Ridge, it is just a stone's throw from Edge, where my mother was born. Both are suburbs of Hearne, Texas. His parents, Olga and Conard, and his seven brothers and sisters lived off the land in more ways than one.

As a young boy, my father experienced many a morning when his father would set the plow and set off for a day of oil speculating, hoping to buy that one piece of land that would gush forth bountiful crude and plentiful riches. My grandfather spent his life searching for that elusive fortune, buying and selling land, negotiating mineral rights, raiding the family piggy bank, hoping against all hope for a fast buck and get-rich-quick strike at the end of a drill bit in the Post Oak region of East Central Texas. Meanwhile, my father and his mother would spend the better part of the day behind a mule following that plow, preparing the land to provide the family's sustenance for that season and beyond. The collard greens, hen eggs, and corn on the cob were supplemented with a steady diet of possum stew and squirrel dumplings. Such fare seemed substantial enough, however, for my father and his siblings. "We ate well," my father remembered, "but we never had a dime."

"I didn't know they made children's shoes till I got to the first grade," he would typically add, probably more for modern-day effect than historical accuracy.

My father learned some valuable lifelong lessons in those fields, as he persevered behind the plow and the mule that would eventually serve as his school bus. His core values were shaped early on by the endless afternoons with his brothers hunting possum and squirrel along the Brazos River bottomlands. Preparation. Perseverance. Hard work. Hanging in for the long haul. Making a little go a long way. Seeing something through to the end. As Jesus once ironically told the young man who wouldn't drop everything and follow, "No one who puts a hand to the plow and looks back is fit for the kingdom of God." My father kept a hand to the plow his entire life, and he will be remembered as a responsible and generous provider.

His father died a poor man. "Our grandfather was basically just a sharecropper," my brother claims, rather pejoratively. I'd rather think of him as a speculator. Which is probably why my father was not. Which is probably why I am. A speculator—of the spiritual sort.

Early in my adolescence, I accompanied my mother and father on a family trip to a friend's ranch on the edge of the Texas Hill Country, near the town of Luling. We had the whole place to ourselves for a week. It was a sprawling but homey spread, centered by a ranch house with a big lap of a porch. The lush lawn was shaded by the protective, outstretched limbs of stooped-over, grandfatherly live oaks. A garden flourished there where we could pick our own tomatoes and okra. Just beyond the lawn was a refreshing, spring-fed swimming hole. I would float for hours on those scorching summer afternoons trying to ignore the occasional snake that slid by.

And there were horses, a whole pasture full of 'em. "You catch 'em, you ride 'em," Smitty, the owner, had told us. My father showed me how to catch one with a bucket of oats. He also demonstrated how, using his country-boy tact, he could entice a steed to trust his country-boy tack. Without regard for equestrian etiquette, my father would yank open Mrs. Mare's mouth to shove in bit, bridle, and reins, throw a blanket on her, and strap on a saddle faster than she could say, "Nay." After all those years of collaborating with a mule, which is basically a half-horse with a learning disability and a bad attitude, this here was mere horseplay.

We even got my mother on a horse on that trip. She never quite figured out that it was possible for her to make a horse move or change direction, but she looked quite content simply sitting patiently on her saddle while her horse grazed for half an hour.

While she may not have actually ridden a horse, she could still boast of having sat upon one for an extended period of time. I still have a picture of this momentous occasion—proving that despite the herbivorous feast occurring beneath her, she maintained excellent posture, and her scarf stayed in place throughout the entire ordeal!

Wading through untamed underbrush up to our necks, we could see the blue-green waters of the Colorado River flow lazily past an old mill on the periphery of the property. The true gem, however, as far as my father was concerned, was a muddy creek hidden by thicket, slowly winding its way through the heart of the ranch. Its waters teemed with catfish the size of baby calves; its banks abounded with wildlife of every sort. Plodding along in a patched-up, poor excuse for a rowboat, armed with a shotgun and enough trot line to deplete a small ocean, my father set out to stalk his prey.

It was a country-boy's Eden. Every trot line hooked a hearty fat cat with well-groomed whiskers. Such abundant waters may as well have been stocked; you could almost reach in and pull out your dream fish. Not content with the hundred pounds of fish flesh already strewn around the boat bottom, the all-powerful fisherman quickly transformed into the mighty hunter as he spotted unsuspecting squirrels in the trees above.

As a very young boy, I was filled with a naïve joy and delight when my father once brought me a squirrel tail from a hunting trip. My mother was less than thrilled with such bounty, and refused to acknowledge his kill as meat and prepare it as a meal. I ran around the neighborhood waving my prize at my awe-struck peers. I certainly recognized that possession of a squirrel tail was not quite in the same league as the coonskin courage of a Daniel Boone cap, but it was close enough for me and my friends.

The dawn of adolescence had made me more apprehensive of such acts and more appreciative of the relationship between the tail and the rest of the squirrel. My uneasiness spread to a hollow, gut-wrenching sickness as I watched my father, on that summer afternoon, load his rifle and take aim at the life of what I regarded as an innocent creature. Outrage over such an injustice ran up and down my spine and before I knew it, I blurted out, "Don't kill him!"

My father looked at me like I had just asked him for a bong hit on behalf of a gay lover.

"Do not kill the squirrel," I repeated forcefully. I felt a surge of manhood fortify my stance.

He took aim anyway.

Call it individuation. Call it retribution. Call it moral outrage. Call it the call of the wild. Call it sheer stupidity. I shouted, "No!" and brazenly reached across the boat and seized the barrel of the gun, attempting to confiscate the weapon. We could've been killed for the sake of a member of the rodent family.

It was a moment of insanity—or ultimate liberation. He shoved me aside with the butt of his rifle and raised his voice in a commanding crescendo: "Let go!"

I did. For a long time.

Like Jacob and the angel who wrestled at the river Jabbok, we both left that battle wounded. But unlike Jacob, it would be years before I would get my blessing.

Perhaps it was overblown in my adolescent mind at the time. But that soft thud of an innocent creature's body landing between my feet parted the family waters as wide as Moses' parting of the Red Sea. There was a deep chasm between us now. Father and son sat in silence as he rowed us back upstream to the place where we had put in. My thoughts and emotions alternated between exhilaration and penitence, confusion and certainty, solidarity and isolation. With one shot he had killed a part of me, but another part was awkwardly stirring within, waiting to be born.

Back at the ranch house, I recognized the cold, hard fact that my father and I were different. Our values and our paths would diverge, and a thousand squirrel tails could not bring me back into the fold.

Over the years, my father and I went our separate ways. He continued his squirrel-hunting habits, even in the big city. He would patiently await them on his back porch and pick them off his backyard pecan trees with a single shot. "How dare they mess with my pecans," he'd say, justifying his slaughter to no one in particular. Although he could certainly afford whatever he wanted at the grocery store, he continued to scour the metropolitan landscape for sustenance. There was not a wild berry patch or an unclaimed pecan grove anywhere within the city limits that he hadn't harvested. A sort of urban sharecropper, he turned out to be. But he shared his bounty with everyone.

I chose the spiritual path and eventually became an Episcopal priest, a far trek from my fundamentalist upbringing. It is difficult for an outsider to fathom the trauma such a turn created for my family. "I know your parents must be proud," unsuspecting well-wishers would offer.

I did not want to spend an hour explaining that my family comes from a small, obscure denomination that didn't exist until the nineteenth century and is confined mainly to the southern United States. Although these people are not even a blip on the radar screen of religion, they remain so insular and tight-minded that they actually insist they are the sole possessors and purveyors of God's truth. Anyone who doesn't see it or do it their way is not only wrong, but damned for all eternity.

To such well-intended remarks, I would usually simply respond, "I'm sure they are." Although I am quite sure they were not.

A few years after my divorce and my ordination (events that were, in my family's eyes, unfortunate and unforgivable, in that order), my mother and Rachel, my girlfriend at the time, were viewing old family photos. A photo from my ordination day appeared. My mother held it askance as if it were in dire need of ritual, medical, and moral cleansing. Mom mournfully reflected, "Of course we were all devastated when Bill told us he was becoming an Episcopal priest." Seemingly holding back tears, she added pensively, "But you know, I guess there are worse things."

I am fond of telling my close friends that my parents would have been *disappointed* had I become a pimp, but they were *devastated* that I became a priest. Rachel and I still laugh about my mother's observations, but sometimes my laughter is halfhearted, concealing my own disappointment and devastation.

I am comforted, however, by the scriptures we share. As the Apostle said, "Work out your own salvation with fear and trembling." Find your own way, he seems to say. Choose the path that is true for you, the road that calls from deep within, that seems honest and, finally, familiar. The way that leads genuinely home. The way that won't be easy.

"It's a long road home," I once penned for a country-western song, "longer than all of my dreams. It's a long road home—but I know it's where I should be." Authenticity seems to be the ultimate test. If there is a question posed at Heaven's gate, I believe it will simply be whether we were courageous enough to live out our unique God-given identities. "William, were you William?" God will ask.

I am certain of nothing in this life. But I am well aware that if the speculator in each one of us has been working overtime, we will not be far from our true selves and from trusting our true selves. Hopefully not far from the kingdom, either. Speculation can be defined as meditation and reflection, or it can refer to a risky business venture. For my money, they're the same thing. And if we arrive home only to discover that we've come full circle—well, I guess there are worse things. At least we'll know for sure where we are—and where we've been.

It is much later now. And I am much different. Though not too much. It is almost thirty years after the Luling Squirrel Massacre. I am not a pure pacifist anymore. I recognize that my father and I are more alike than unalike, and that the sharecropper and the speculator may be one.

During his later years, my father and I became closer, particularly after my mother's death from cancer. Though he never would receive communion from me, he sat through a service or two without the physical compulsion of a straitjacket. He even managed to mumble, "You said some nice things today," after a Father's Day service in which I held him up as an example. And while he could not fathom the idea of a dog who lived indoors, he would occasionally ask about his granddog, Sam.

Once he even spent the night with me in Austin while he was on his way to Abilene for a religious conference. He slept downstairs on the couch, while Sam attempted to bond with him by sleeping on the floor nearby. (Sam was used to being addressed by name; the best my dad could do was, "Gitdowndog.") In the middle of the night, my father got up to empty his bladder. Sam decided he would endear himself to his grandfather by crawling up on the couch and keeping his place nice and toasty while he was gone. As far as my father was concerned, Sam's act was most inhospitable. He may as well have pooped on his pillow.

The next morning my father growled, "Do you know what that rascal did last night?" accusing Sam of the high crime of temporary occupation of a warm spot. My father never stayed with me again. However, Rachel and I now preface accounts of Sam's activities with our new favorite question, "Do you know what that rascal did?" Sam and I continue to take pride in our mutual rascality, especially in the presence of those irascible ones. It loosens them up, we hope.

After that, my visits with my father were on his turf and terms, without Sam. I looked forward to our visits in Houston, which would usually include a breakfast or lunch at the Country Kitchen. The Country Kitchen was a place where our worlds collided and integrated, so we could break bread together. I think it reminded him of the country while, ironically, it reminded me of the city. And we both liked the food. While it may not be Spago or Tavern on the Green (or Denny's for that matter), the Country Kitchen is my kind of establishment. Located just a few blocks from my dad's house in a basically blue-collar, ethnically diverse part of town, it's the kind of place where the waitress greets you in Spanish, but still calls you "honey" with a Texas accent, where heavily tattooed, jewelry-encrusted gang members share space with retired Rotarians, where $1.99 will get you the best biscuits and gravy that side of Tomball, and for lunch, $4.99 will buy you a Big Texan—two meats, four vegetables, and all the homemade rolls you can eat.

My father and I never engaged in what you would call extensive conversation, but much of what we did say was said at the Country Kitchen. It was there we talked about his struggle with cancer, my travel adventures overseas, his rapidly changing church, and the latest developments in my often entertaining love life. And it was where he talked of what might have been when he confided that if he had won his battle with cancer, he could have married JoAnn, his wonderful lady friend of several years.

In those last months at the Country Kitchen, we ignored Miss Manners and my aversion to any public display of piety, planted our elbows firmly on the table, grasped each other's hands, and prayed together, out loud, most fervently. There we gave thanks for the food and blessings of this life, and asked quite specifically for several more years for my father on this earth. When we would pray, it was not uncommon for the tough guys on either side of us—the survey crews, roughnecks, rappers, and cops—to bow their heads too, as a kind of Country Kitchen courtesy.

Although my father was losing his battle with cancer, he and JoAnn got married anyway, much to our family's delight. The simple afternoon ceremony in her backyard concluded quickly. My father had told the minister prior to the service, "Just get to the point." Their reception, shared with one other couple, consisted of sandwiches, fruit, and iced tea. For a honeymoon, my brother had offered his condo in Grand Cayman, while I suggested they should at least book a suite in the Four Seasons on the Lake in Austin.

"I don't have real fancy tastes," my father had reminded me on more than one occasion.

Ignoring our advice, they drove to College Station and stayed at the Ramada Inn. The next day they toured the Bush Presidential Library. "Something we've been wanting to do," he said. Then he ventured up the road to Hearne to say "howdy" and introduce his bride to his brothers and sisters. It wasn't my idea of a honeymoon, but for some reason, it sure seemed right.

Knowing the gravity of my father's condition, his church held a dinner in his honor shortly thereafter. As a tribute, I wrote the following poem. I realized as I wrote it that our differences, although significant, were now irrelevant. He had taught me nothing about the finer things in life, but he had taught me everything about the better things in life.

A Man I Know

There is a man I know
whose convictions run deep,
whose kindness holds fast,
whose generosity reaches forth,
whose love embraces all. **He is my father.**

There is a place I recall   where action speaks louder (and wiser) than the reticent word. Where the Cokes are cold, the hot-sauce is homemade, the lemons are from the backyard; where the peas are fresh-shelled, the blackberries picked by hand, the pecans cracked from a grafted tree; the fish caught with a brother or a grandson; where the cornbread dressing is the best anyone has ever tasted; where breakfast always awaits you in the morning even when the cook has no appetite or desire.   **It is home.**

There is a holiday I remember   when as a young boy I was awakened early by strong, tender hands. We drove silently together to a strange house, on an unknown street, in an unfamiliar part of town, where the two of us delivered sustenance and joy to a family unlike ours. I missed the parade that year. But I understood the meaning of gratitude for the first time, and I am thankful to this day.   **It was Thanksgiving.**

There is a picture I display   proudly on my mantle. where I now live and move and have my being. Wherein a young man in his early 20s, smartly dressed in an Air Force uniform, bears a striking resemblance to Elvis Presley—only more handsome! Virtually every female who has ever laid eyes on that picture asks, "Who is that?" and when I tell them nearly always add, "Your dad is fine—what happened to you?"   **That's my dad.**

There is a calling I experience   whereby the gospel becomes real, and present, and tangible. A service rendered to the world in the name of God, a holy beckoning to seek and serve Christ in all persons, inspired by one for whom the kingdom of heaven was, and is, ultimate reality. Many was the night he'd be out "herding sheep" past my bedtime. And we learned there are priority covenants, higher callings, preferential truths. How many lives have been touched by such selfless compassion, such genuine other-centered living? There are countless sheep who have been brought into the fold of God because of him and his influence.

                    He is a shepherd.

There is a hope I embrace   both here and in the life to come, because of his example. The capacity to endure, the audacity to desire (even in the face of despair), the faith to engage in a new beginning when the end would seem imminent. I believe, primarily because   **He is a believer.**

And there is a grace I cherish,   a gift to share, a blessing to bestow because I have known such generosity in him.

I am amazed by his grace, gift, and blessing. The Christmas presents. The birthday dinners. The trips taken. The checks written. The faith imparted. Hospitality. Humility. Goodness. Love.

I am blessed.

Yes, there is a man I know
whose convictions run deep,
whose kindness holds fast,
whose generosity reaches forth,
whose love embraces all.   **He is my father.**

There is a man I know
And from him
I know
what it is
to be
a man.

Through the poem I had made my penultimate peace and said what I needed to say. Yet one thing was painfully absent: my father's blessing. As Jacob limped forever after Jabbok, so that wound from our creek battle, although no longer raw, was still tender. I was not naïve enough to assume that he could ever wholeheartedly endorse my way of connecting with the world and my Creator, but I still longed for some simple touch from him and the acknowledgment that he was with me, even from afar. I grieved and resigned myself to the inevitable reality that I would never receive such a thing. He had missed my final Sunday at St. James in Austin and with it, I thought, his final opportunity for a belated affirmation, if not blessing. After seven and a half years at a wonderful, multicultural church, I had recently announced my resignation. The church planned a gala farewell service on December 13, 1998, and all my friends and family were invited. All came—except for him.

When I went home for Christmas, I was acutely aware of his worsening condition. He had deteriorated to the point where he could barely get about. I told my brother we should, as a family, accompany my father to his church on Sunday, as it might be our last chance to do so together. Sure enough, he struggled mightily just to make it into his pew. He was too weak to sing. For the first time in my life, I missed his wide bass voice as it floundered around the lower register on every hymn, always a quarter step flat and always louder than everyone else's. He slept through the sermon.

As the congregation formed a circle to welcome the newly baptized, we made our way outside. My father took a few steps, haltingly, and then stopped to survey the family. Even a man from a nonliturgical tradition could recognize the sacramental nature of the moment. He placed a firm hand on my shoulder, just as he had when he baptized me years ago, and gave me a last, resolute look. He said simply, "Well, God bless you, Bill." It was all he said. It was all I needed to hear. The lame could finally walk.

That afternoon, my father and I watched together as our former Houston Oilers, now based in Tennessee, played their last game as the Oilers. Next season, they would be renamed the Tennessee Titans, mythic mostly in their own minds. Appropriately, they lost. The end of another era. Their parents must be disappointed too.

"I guess the day of reckoning has finally come," he told JoAnn the next week, his only allusion to the inevitable. His oncologist asked him if he needed anything. "I guess I need a lot of things," he told the physician, "but I'm not sure you can provide 'em."

Two weeks before he died, as I prepared to return to Austin for a few days, I mentally composed a script of what I wanted to say to him, words of appreciation and gratitude. As I approached his bedside, he opened his eyes, embraced me, and kissed me. I remembered the first feel of those coarse, reassuring whiskers when, as a child, I would press my face against his. Years later, I still felt comforted.

He beat me to the punch by saying, "I appreciate all you've done, Bill."

Realizing I hadn't done much, I simply told the truth. "Well, I appreciate all you've done—you sure have been a good dad to me." I detected a desire on his part to deflect such attention and watched as his face filled with a flush of emotion and a tinge of regret.

His last day of lucidity occurred the day we had set aside to celebrate my birthday. He ate a piece of pizza and a sliver of cake, sat up on the couch in the living room, sang along on "Happy Birthday," and even managed to sign my birthday card. On it he wrote, "I love you you. Dad." I appreciated his remembering the both of me, the one of his raising, and the one of my choosing. It was the last thing he wrote.

I am convinced that his defiance kept him alive longer than he should have been. He complained constantly of constipation and continued to pray over meals until he ran out of breath and could not eat. There were shades of our rowboat battle as he pushed JoAnn and me aside one day when we tried to support him while he stumbled along. "If y'all would just get outta my way," he said, as he sideswiped the kitchen counter. "Well, I'm just not used to . . . you know." Yes, we knew, we understood.

I am told his last word was "no" when the nurse asked, "Are you gonna cooperate and let me put this catheter in?" Good for him. I'm sure he would have said, "Hell, no," had he not been such a religious man.

He had many visitors during those last days. Ralph Engelhardt offered prayer: "God, we've begged and pleaded with you—we don't know what else to do." Obdulio Mendoza reminisced about my father's mentoring him on their mission trips to Central America. Jean Jammer, who grew up in Hearne, brought by a casserole. L. C. Webb sang the simple hymn "God Is So Good." One Sunday, almost a hundred people from his church came en masse to give him an impromptu gospel concert. He always said, "I appreciate your coming by," whether he did or not, and when he grew too weak to speak, he tried his best to indicate that he knew they were there.

But it was George Winfield's visit that I will never forget.

George was a longtime family friend and member of my father's church. He had served as a pallbearer at my mother's funeral five years earlier. George was a slight, less than overpowering man who walked with the aid of a cane. He still had a head full of wavy white hair and was known for his shy, but spacious, smile.

George would often circle the block in his car, slowly, looking to see if someone might be outside, occasionally tooting his horn lightly or pulling up in the driveway, but never violating our space, always keeping a respectful distance. I admire that kind of concern. It doesn't make you put on shoes, sit up straight, and make polite, pretend conversation. But in the end, George couldn't contain himself and figured he'd better stop in before it was too late.

I escorted George to the bedroom and he sat down beside my father, greeting him with, "Bill, it's George." He grabbed my father's limp, almost lifeless hand and shook it because that's what men do. He seemed to search awkwardly for a word of wisdom or endearing phrase with which he might express himself. His shuffling feet and nervous smile betrayed his solicitous state, and he finally admitted, "Bill, I don't know what to say."

I appreciated his honesty, and I felt a solidarity with his predicament. What can one say in the face of death? Words fail us in these moments. Pious platitudes and well-worn clichés are the cheap plastic tools of pedantry. They couldn't plow a sandbox without breaking on first contact with the smallest pebble. A real rabbi would never utter such foolishness.

A prolonged, unwieldy silence enveloped the room. At last, with one final heroic effort to connect, George patted my father on his leg and asked, "Bill, have you eaten any squirrel lately?"

It will forever remain the single most significant question I have ever heard posed to a dying man.

I received news of my father's death on the way home from celebrating my birthday with five buddies in the hip Miami neighborhood of South Beach, a place where velvet ropes separate the sheep from the goats. They know nothing of possums or plows there. Squirrel hunting is both a criminal offense and social suicide. This land of cloned nightclubs, soul-less techno beats, portable trendometers, and paint-by-number beauty could learn a thing or two from the likes of George Winfield. And they've got nothing on the Ramada Inn in College Station.

At the funeral, my brother read a passage of scripture that reminds us, "Nothing can separate us from the love of God." I would need to be reminded. For after I read my father's tribute poem for the last time and took my seat with the rest of the family in the front row, the preacher began a furtive attempt to land a late-round knockout punch.

Luring me into the ring with a squirrel tail as big as my father's life and as broad as my father's dreams, he spoke of diversity, rainbows, and good news for all people. I was about to step aboard the train, when he drew that guilt-laced tail high above his head and slapped me across my surprised face in a final, futile attempt to bring me back into "the one true church."

"Whether you like it or not," he said, glaring right at me. "I know for a fact," he added, "that your father would have wanted it that way."

I made no attempt to disarm him or confiscate his weapon. It had no power over me. I had wrestled at Jabbok and survived. I had said my piece and had my peace. He can have his facts. I'll keep the faith, take my blessing, tuck my tail, and run.

The sharecropper's perseverance and the speculator's explorations eventually paid off. We were surprised to discover that part of the legacy my father left is a royalty check for about forty bucks a month from a gas well in East Central Texas that he inherited from his father. It seems the dinosaur did not die in vain. Although my grandfather did not live to see it, he finally had his day and struck a gusher.

Along the way, I've learned my lessons from both men.

Persevere.

Speculate.

Plow the ground.

But look far beneath the surface too.

And always bless the squirrels.

Before eating.

CHAPTER 10

....

A Reverence for Rabbits

"Fill 'er up, Mr. Miller?"

"Fill 'er up, Rabbit. Sky Chief."

Ah, the dialogue of the gods, the holy alliance of petroleum pontiff and petrol priest, sacerdotal summonings of blessed fuel.

Refinery rep and gasoline guru engage in automotive incantations. Sacramental conduits connect crude and car. Fumes permeate as prayer. The gas tank gurgles an "Amen." The hood bows in obeisance. I am in awe, sitting in the back seat of a brand-new 1965 Oldsmobile.

When I was a young boy, a favorite diversion was to ride with my dad over to the Texaco station on Pinemont Street to fill up the family car with gas. My dad worked for Texaco, so there was the issue of family pride and affirmation. My developing self-esteem needed to know that you could trust your car to the man who wore the star, and so could I trust my life. But more important were our weekly encounters with our favorite service station attendant, a guy named Rabbit.

I cannot overemphasize the significance for a six-year-old to have a big Rabbit service your car. Rabbit was a slight, sure-footed fella who would scamper outta the office and stick his nose up to your car windshield before the bell could clang twice. He had wide, otherworldly gaps between his teeth. He wore a green gasoline shirt with *Rabbit* stitched in cursive red letters above the pocket. I wanted one desperately. For several years I asked Santa for a Rabbit shirt, but he obviously didn't fuel his deer at the Texaco. Too bad the Easter Bunny was limited to candy; he would've understood.

Rabbit became sort of extended family over the years, even after he took over the station. I remember one day Rabbit was busy back in the office and some other guy serviced our car. He will always be a nameless and faceless void, a vehicular vapor, just like all of those "other guys." When it came time to pay, this other guy told my dad they no longer gave double S&H green stamps.

My father the loyal customer, Mr. Texaco, was not happy. He marched right back to the office and asked, "Rabbit, this fella says no more double S&H green stamps. Is that true?"

"No sir, Mr. Miller, not for our good customers. Give Mr. Miller double green stamps," he told the young novice.

We got the double green stamps, but I could see that the world was unraveling. Society was falling apart. Civilization, as we knew it, would soon cease. Uncertainty prevailed, and I feared for our future. That "other guy" was certainly no Rabbit. You see, the fun part was not limited to the gas-getting, for, with your gas, you also got some good stuff like stamps, decals, mugs, toys, tumblers, tickets, and coupons. And if you were really good, as I so often was as a child, your dad bought you an authentic, shiny, red, brand-new Texaco fire truck. Right there. At the gas station. From Rabbit.

In my young mind, meeting Rabbit was not far from meeting God. He was unknown, dark, different. Somewhat mysterious, yet predictably present. We saw him once a week, but never outside the station. He took pride in his work, wore a uniform, and was affiliated with a respectable institution. He filled your tank, cleaned your windshield, and gave you double green stamps. Once I shook his hand. My hand burned a little after that.

There are theologians and philosophers who believe that God changes. And not just from full-serve to self-serve, or from service station to Star Mart. It has nothing to do with consumer trends and customer satisfaction. It's just God's nature, so they say. God is in process. And creation continues even beyond the fossil-fuel era. That's a somewhat scary thought, especially for those whose perceptions of God and the world haven't changed much over the years. And neither have they. But I kind of like that God-view. It makes sense to me and challenges me to do the same, to see myself in process. Another rabbit revealed such truth when I was much older.

It was an Easter miracle actually. I know, I know. Bunnies have no place in the Easter liturgy, but this one refused to be denied. It was another sign that the sacred and the secular are Siamese twins who refuse to be separated. This visitation was surely an Easter miracle.

It was customary at my church in Austin to hire a large human to dress up in a pink bunny costume and hide eggs for the children after the Easter service. I had mixed feelings about this liturgical innovation, but the children loved looking for eggs with ol' E.B., and I enjoyed having my picture taken with a rabbit once a year (it lowers the blood pressure).

On this particular Easter, the rabbit was late and could not be introduced during announcement time. The children suspected that the traditionalists had kidnapped him and pummeled him to death with 1928 prayer books. I suspected that he was probably just slow to get his furry butt out of bed and would be there before the service ended.

We were all surprised, however, as I turned around to face the altar for the mass and saw just outside the large window, standing up on his hind legs, the biggest, softest, real-live rabbit this side of Bunnyland. His appearance was as unreal and unpredictable as, say, a resurrection.

He stayed there throughout the Easter mass, occasionally wandering around the grassy area behind the altar, sniffing, nibbling, glancing. As soon as the service ended he disappeared into a patch of woods near the creek out back.

Throughout the Easter season, for the next six weeks that rabbit showed up for every service, even the 7:30 a.m. Wednesday service.

I got a call one week from a neighbor. "Is that the church's rabbit I keep seeing?" she asked.

"Not exactly," I told her, "although his service attendance has been more faithful that 90 percent of our membership." I secretly hoped to slip him a pledge card.

No one in the neighborhood knew where he came from. No one ever got close enough to touch him. He proved quite elusive. I brought Sam up to greet him one day, and as soon as he spotted Sam, he was outta there faster than a hungry agnostic on Super Bowl Sunday. This bunny was an animal enigma. We could not capture or corral him. We knew he was there, and we knew he'd been there, more by traces and tracks than personal encounters. A partially burrowed hole. A broken twig. A flattened blade. He always lurked just outside the sanctuary but seemed to take an interest in what went on inside. What joy he brought to St. James! There was some inexplicable sense of the divine presence whenever he showed up. Still, I had my doubts about his divinity.

That is, until he was killed by a pack of wild dogs. Just behind the altar. Nearest the tabernacle that contains the Blessed Sacrament. A woman from the church had gone by early one morning to check on the volunteer training schedule for the Center for Battered Women. She called me in tears. I buried him that morning in a shallow grave visible from every vantage point in the sanctuary space. As I turned the blunt earth over, my own tears baptized that bunny and marked him as Christ's own forever.

The Easter season was officially over. We were now in the season of Pentecost, also called Ordinary Time. Real Time. The place where most of us live and move and have our being, and bunnies do not. Where God is often uninvited. And if he gets too close, we just might kill him. It would not be the first time.

Children in festive finery flower the cross on Easter Day. They stay home on Good Friday. But Easter miracles must have an element of Good Friday within them, or they would resound with all the hollowness of a gas station gong on a long deserted highway. These are hard truths. Hard rabbit truths. And we must not tell the children. Yet. That God does not eat from our hand.

The times change. My dad started buying whatever gas was cheapest. I'm a Chevron man myself. And God has grown up. He no longer scampers when I pull up. Doesn't wear a uniform. Isn't aligned with a particular company. Always eludes my grasp when I try to shake his hand. And all of us continue to evolve. But I still brake for bunnies. And keep searching for God. It's quite a long trek.

Fill 'er up, Rabbit.

PART TWO

··············

Midlife Crises

············

CHAPTER 11

Bare-Naked Bellies

They say that a dog will not turn over on his back and expose his underside unless he truly trusts you. In Sam's case, such behavior has less to do with interpersonal integrity than with the intense desire to be scratched on his belly. If Sam is in the mood for an accelerated stomach claw, he will roll over and flash anyone within eyesight. Sam displays his "Come on in! We're open!" sign with no shame whatsoever. Front paws up and back, around his ears. Hind legs out and away, forming a *V* for vacancy. Sam sticks his head up over the furry horizon and scans the room for approaching fingernails. "All human hands cleared for landing," he woofs hopefully.

It is more and more rare in my own life to solicit a belly scratch from friends or bystanders. For as I have grown older, I have fought an increasingly ugly battle with my bulging paunch. My waistline has grown faster than my wisdom. A medical doctor in my congregation once approached me after a service and offered an unsolicited diagnosis of a condition he was most concerned about. "It appears you have Dunlop disease, Father." Fearful of the possibly life-threatening implications, I asked for elaboration. "Well, it looks to me like your belly dunlopped over your belt." An ex-girlfriend was even more direct, patting my middle and inquiring, "So when is it due?"

But the true spiritual community is more like a lounge than a gym. Abs of steel, which will eventually rust anyway, are not necessary for membership. No waxing, buffing, peeling, primping, shaving, or laser treatments required. There is no need to suck in our guts when God walks by. Pooches and paunches—of all sizes, sorts, and conditions—are allowed.

Sam's openness, trust, and self-effacing acknowledgment that he needs a good scratching remind me of the ultimate gift God has to offer: grace. And the only way we can receive it—with openness and trust, admitting our deep need, willing to assume a downright goofy position. Sunny-side down. Dirty-side up. Hairy, flabby, dunlopped bellies exposed.

Once I led a mission trip for young people in my church to the Texas coastal town of Galveston. One evening, after a long day's work at a local community center, we decided we'd have a little fun and play miniature golf. The large putting course was perched on a small hill overlooking a sea wall. A nautical theme prevailed: towering pirates, watchful sea lions, menacing shark jaws. Playing just ahead of us was a young boy who appeared to be about five years old, accompanied by an older gentleman, perhaps his father. He was a crusty, weathered sort of man who looked like he might spend the day at sea—a sailor or a shrimper, perhaps. We waited for them to finish the windmill hole—where your timing must help your ball avoid the rotating vanes that try to prevent your putt from reaching the other side.

We waited longer than a fisherman who's unknowingly lost his bait.

The young boy was not having much success. The unforgiving windmill swatted his ball back toward the tee at least a dozen times. Finally, he just picked up the ball and pitched it between the blades. When he got to the hole side of the green, he resumed his putting attack, ricocheting his ball off of nearby benches, innocent bystanders, and other nonhazards. His shots careened off embankments, giant shrimp tails, and the lobster with a six-shooter on neighboring holes, until he finally managed to sink a putt. At that moment, he thrust his putter into the air and shouted, "A two!"

The old seafarer's lips crinkled into a big smile and he said, "Now you know you didn't get a two."

At that, the little boy looked right up at him, recognizing the mess he'd made of the hole, a bogey to the fourth power, as close to par as a distant galaxy is to Earth, and asked, "Would you *give* me a two?"

I believe it was Jung who said, "The brighter the halo, the smellier the feet." For even the best among us have gone to the dogs. If the truth be told, we've made a mess of most of the course, and we miss the mark more often than not. There's no use pretending we even belong at the tee. Nonetheless, for some strange reason, God can be trusted to look down and write on the only scorecard that matters—an undeserved, unmerited, unbelievable—PAR. God cheats on our behalf and gives us a two. "My grace is sufficient," God has said.

We call tangible expressions of such grace the sacraments. Sacraments happen when an ordinary item or occasion—say water, or wine, or a human touch—is infused with grace from above and becomes a common conduit for extraordinary love, putting a human face on divine initiative. The two most important sacraments have traditionally been Baptism and Eucharist, occasions that initiate us into and sustain us within the kingdom. There are other recognized sacraments, too, such as confirmation, healing, and matrimony. There are unrecognized ones as well, for the truth is that there are as many sacraments as there are opportunities to impart grace. In other words, they are limitless. Someone has said that most of the recognized sacraments can be reduced to three basics: a bath, a meal, and a hug. Add a good scratching to that list, and what more could anyone need?

To receive the sacraments does not require any special qualifications or superhuman powers on our parts, just some old-fashioned honesty, vulnerability, and openness. We don't always have to spread our legs like Sam, but we do have to open our hearts and expose our deepest selves and needs. To be cleansed is to admit we are dirty. To be fed is to admit we are hungry. To be hugged is to admit we crave affection and attention.

Beginning at age three, I spent every Friday night with my second set of parents, Rosemary and Hank Bartos. They lived across the street from us on West Thirtieth Street, and they were everything my family was not. They cussed, drank, and had a boat. They sang along with the piano player at the local pizza parlor. They listened to Willie Nelson and watched NASCAR on television. Hank smoked cigars and called me a "mullet." They were devout Catholics. I learned to play bingo, drink beer, float down Texas rivers, and inhale the mystery that is church under their tutelage. And I am grateful.

Every Friday for nine years, I made the forty-foot trek to their front door carrying a small, square pink suitcase with a palm tree on it. Inside was exactly one pair of underwear. In later years, I added a bowling ball to the briefs, since we had begun to go bowling every Saturday morning. And I don't recall ever lacking a thing.

Rosemary and Hank always supplied provisions and a place to play at my own pace. On each visit, I knew that I would find at least one well-stocked cookie jar in the lower cupboard, well within my reach. I could rest assured that Hank would not place a "Keep Out" sign amidst his prized lighter collection, where I'd wage war with the plastic toy soldiers they kept in stock, waiting for my arrival. I trusted them with the truth about myself, even when it wasn't all that adorable. I could wet the bed there and not be made to feel ashamed. Rosemary just changed the sheets. It was a sacramental kind of place where common cookies and cheap toy soldiers were infused with grace, a sacred alternative to the drab fundamentalism that could sometimes suck the life out of any space. And I learned that you don't need to take much with you when you travel, and you can be at home even in a place that is not your primary residence.

My Uncle Charlie still teases me about the time he and his wife Judy and my three cousins showed up unannounced on their way to a weekend at the beach. They asked if I could accompany them. My mom, anxious to get rid of me at any opportunity, said, "Billy, go pack your bag." When we got to the modest little motel just across the street from the breakers, my uncle's entire family hooted and hollered as I unpacked my two items: a swimsuit and a toothbrush. Such a spartan suitcase may have actually contributed to one of the fondest trips I recall from my childhood.

I have learned over the years that the one who has the most toys usually loses. Our true needs are but few. Grace and graceful people supply them all. We don't have to have all that much to be satisfied and whole. Through grace, we can pack light and come as we are. When I pick up Sam at Rachel's apartment each week, he brings one bone and one toy—anything more is distracting, even confusing. Too much stuff is the cause of so much misery.

Even in a small apartment, there is room enough to provide for all of Sam's various moods. Sam has particular places he occupies depending on his needs. When he's feeling somewhat threatened, he hides under the bed, or wedges himself between the ottomans, havens not unlike the sheet-covered forts we erected in the corners of our bedrooms as children. If it's refreshment he seeks, he'll sprawl on the hard, cool floor of the kitchen or bathroom, or rest his head on the windowsill to catch a breeze. If it's comfort he's after, he'll embed himself among the pillows on the couch or even crawl into bed with me and straddle my entire body so I cannot breathe. I allow him the freedom to choose whatever position suits him, instead of forcing him into particular places based on my own preferences, comfort, or convenience.

The church should offer the same such places for anybody who seeks them. Unfortunately, we are better at making others conform to our own requirements than adapting a space to the spiritual needs of others. No shirt, no shoes, no spirituality, the judging church seems to say. It is no wonder that among religious people I have sometimes felt like the animal in the "which one doesn't belong?" portion of our kindergarten workbooks. Given a picture of a pear, an apple, a banana, and a goat, our assignment was to circle the one that does not belong. Guess which one I am?

In the fellowship of Christ, however, no one gets marked as not belonging, easily discarded, or told to cover up what might be considered offensive. It is a haven of safety, security, refreshment, and comfort. A sanctuary in which we can be ourselves, be vulnerable, and still belong. It is a makeshift fort off in a corner of the world where we need no defenses, barriers, or walls. Only our pretensions will deny us membership. We can go there topless, or at least bare-bellied, and no one stares, or attempts to remove the lint from our navels.

Years ago at a rather large, sophisticated urban parish in the museum district of a southern city, a homeless man became irritated in the hallway near the administrative offices. Apparently, he didn't get exactly what he had requested in the way of financial assistance from the parish staff. He began to make a scene, firing a vitriolic spray of expletives in a loud voice, letting loose a barrage of profanity right there before God and the church secretary. The church custodian, a good-hearted, no-nonsense, not particularly well-educated man, heard as much as he could stand. He walked right up to the man in the midst of his diatribe, shook his finger in his face, and warned him in no uncertain terms, "Listen buddy, this here's a church, and we don't use none of that *pro-found* language around here!" Would that it were true.

Engaging in the great cover-up of "profundity," we hide the profane truth about ourselves, the truth that could set us free, and find some much-needed but hardly deserved grace. For most people don't give a damn what we profess. What they want to know is, can I trust you? If I expose my belly in your presence, will you laugh, vomit, call the police, hit me, or demand that I go on a diet? Or will you scratch me? Lovingly. Patiently. Tenderly. A little harder and to the right.

If so, at last, I am home.

CHAPTER 12

············

Dust Devils

Remember that you are dust, and to dust you shall return.
BOOK OF COMMON PRAYER, ASH WEDNESDAY

Her name is Angelica. This wee lass of a pup looks like Christmas—a cross between that heavenly tasting candy we call divinity and a lace-draped, cheery angel as pure as the driven snow. A teeny bundle of joy, weighing in at a cuddly five pounds, Angelica is a milky-white Maltese with soft, cute curls and sweet Christian parents (they even have a fish symbol on their car). She could pass for Lamb Chop's baby girl, so adorable is this pearly faced hand-puppet.

Do not be deceived.

Angelica she is not. Demonica, or even Satanica, perhaps. This mean little shrill-pitched snippet of terror is all Judgment Day, Armageddon, and Sheol rolled into one. Penance and piss on a leash. Brimstone, hellfire, and damnation lurk just behind those curls. She is as innocent as an unsuspected paper cut. This lovely little lady's complexion reflects more ashen horror than ivory purity. She is the wet dog blanket of neighborhood walks, and Sam, all eighty-two pounds of him, steers clear of her house every chance he gets.

Making a wide berth upon our approach, Sam prefers to take his chances with the two-ton pickup trucks racing down Ninth Street rather than tangle with the jalapeño-hearted vixen. Without the slightest provocation, Angelica will jump up, track Sam down, and sink her cherub-sized teeth into Sam's unsuspecting schnozz. She is a shark in sheep's clothing.

I have watched Sam chase horses ten times his size around a pasture, but get within a half-block of doll-sized Angelica's house, and Sam will slam on the brakes with enough force to stop the Space Shuttle. Angelica will shake with stroke-inducing tremors if Sam is within eyesight or earshot and she is not set free to launch a virulent and violent attack.

Now that I am about to be sued for libel by Angelica's parents, let me point out that I am not the one without sin casting stones. Sam is no saint either. While he is not violent or aggressive, he has exhibited slothful, gluttonous, and selfish behavior on more than one occasion. Not to mention the countless times he has passed gas in an enclosed area. Typically, when someone else screws up, we call it "sin." When I screw up, I call it "an honest mistake." Sin or mistake, angelic or satanic, overt or covert, the bottom line is we all fall short.

Once, at a summer Bible camp for economically disadvantaged children, a teacher tried to illustrate this point by quoting the Bible verse which states that even our righteousness is a filthy rag in the sight of God. The teacher, relying on the powerful symbol of the object lesson, held up an especially dirty dishcloth, soiled with all sorts of dark matter. "This is us, children," she said. "We are all filthy rags," at which point a young man, who had a hard enough life growing up in a government housing project, sprang to his feet and shouted, "I ain't no filthy rag!" Well I ain't no filthy rag either, but all of us, including Angelica and Sam, do get a bit dusty, if not dirty at times, and are in dire need of a reprimand, a reorientation, or even a good old-fashioned bath.

Though she most assuredly possesses some measure of sweetness and light, Angelica reminds me of what it's like to be fluffy on the outside and crunchy on the inside, to have a soft exterior and a hard interior, to be surrounded by icing and filled with crap. And she reminds me that evil comes in all colors, species, shapes, and sizes. Evil is not always packaged as an overtly menacing, in-your-face, skyscraper-sized monster. It is possible for the fluffiest, undersized poofballs to be possessed by the deadliest of demons. Such diminutive details can strike when we least suspect. To recognize evil and acknowledge its reality in the world and within ourselves is the first step toward eradicating, or at least diminishing, its influence.

Our baptismal vows place an equal emphasis on turning toward the good and turning away from the bad, on embracing the godly and renouncing the forces of wickedness, on following Christ and fleeing the devil. If such antiquated terminology doesn't work for you, that's no big deal. The point is to recognize the reality of evil—that it is real, present, hurtful, and closer to home than we might think. And that it sometimes seems to be a deeply embedded force, with a life and a will of its own, biting someone's nose with sharp teeth, injuring their hearts with hurtful words, eating all the dog food, or staking a claim to something that is not rightfully its own. It is wrong, and it is to be acknowledged, confronted, rejected, and corrected.

Though it is certainly politically correct, socially acceptable, psychologically expedient, and perhaps culturally hip to merely accentuate the positive and pretend the negative is nonexistent, the world contains both—and so do we. It is sometimes a wonderful world, as Louis Armstrong reminds us. It is sometimes a big ol' goofy world, as John Prine reminds us. And it sometimes downright sucks, as Beavis and Butthead remind us. To ignore the cold and hard and embrace only the warm and fuzzy is not to do anyone a favor. For I'm not okay and you're not okay, and that is not necessarily okay. Denying the reality and distorting the truth will come back to bite us every time.

My very first experience with a dog was the sweet collie who lived in the doghouse just beyond my backyard when I was a young child. Her name was Tammy, and she had the privilege of eating the table scraps of the lovely Czechoslovakian woman who lived right behind us. Mrs. Syptak made the best cakes, pies, kolaches, and stews I have ever tasted, and always delivered some sort of tempting homemade surprise to our backdoor on birthdays, holidays, or whenever a fresh batch of pastries necessitated immediate consumption. To say that her dog Tammy ate well is to say that the New York Yankees have had some success on the field. Such a diet led to a sort of perpetual state of lethargic bliss. Tammy was content to sleep or not, fetch or not, go for a walk or not, to be petted or not. She would usually acknowledge my presence by opening one eye, halfway. She went with the flow, accommodating whatever mood whatever human near her might happen to be in. I enjoyed our always pleasant encounters and assumed that all dogs were so easygoing and nice.

I was wrong. My second canine experience occurred when I went over to Craig Enoch's house to play football on his lawn. His dog, a runt resembling a sausage with four tiny duck feet, was chained to a doghouse in his backyard (and it was a rather long chain, I might add). As I nonchalantly approached this teeny-weenie of a dog to give him a friendly pat on the head, the spicy little link ran after me and chomped down on my left calf, removing a significant portion of what had been my leg. After the initial shock of having teeth embedded in my skin wore off, I ran screaming all the way home.

"I got bit by a dog!" I kept yelling, trying to convince myself of a reality I could not imagine, even after my mother called the doctor, summoned my older brother for support, and whisked me into the car. As we backed out of the driveway, who should be waiting at the curb but Craig Enoch, football still tucked under his right arm. My mother rolled down her car window to hear Craig state in a rather unemotional tone of voice, "I just wanted to make sure Billy was okay." My mother, who does not do well with flat affects when emotional extremes are called for, exhibited a rare display of profanity, and screamed, "Hell no, Billy's not okay. He just got bit by the damned dog!" She then shoved her accelerator to the floor and left little Craig staring at a trail of muffler smoke.

Later that evening, Craig's father came by to assure us that the dog never bit and had all of his shots. He apologized for the dog's most unusual and unexpected behavior. I was back playing football the next day—but not in Craig's backyard—and I steered clear of dogs for years. From that day forward I reasoned that a dog by any other name could still bite as hard. And that shots are a good idea. For all of us.

I suppose it is generally proper to put a positive spin on most creatures. I nonetheless wonder if we are sometimes tying bows on turds. If criticism is to be truly constructive, some demolition and rebuilding is in order. So many times I have heard, "You know, deep down, he's really a good person" when we all suspect that deep down he's really a bigger jackass than any of us ever imagined. Sometimes it takes a loose cannon like John the Baptist or some other prophet to shoot from the hip and into the heart and call us what we are—or sometimes can be—a brood of vipers, a bunch of hypocrites, human beings who desperately need to change. To help us courageously admit, "No, I am not alright. I've been bitten or have bitten or will bite, and I am in need of a physician, a shrink, a priest, or a shot." Exorcism may no longer be in fashion and today's demons may be dressed up and downplayed, but their teeth are still sharp, and they still lurk in perfectly respectful places—and people.

Several years ago, one of my former students, now a pediatrician in Hollywood, Bart Rountree, set off on a Latin American expedition before buckling down for medical school. He wrote to me from western Guatemala about an experience he had had a few days earlier in a small Mexican town called Cholula, a town populated by a very proud indigenous people who kicked the Catholics out in the 1850s and continue to maintain their ancient Mayan practices. There is one modern addition, however, Bart wrote: Pepsi Cola! Apparently the people of Cholula believe that burping expels evil spirits and when Pepsi was brought to the town in 1972, it was considered a gift from the gods. Bart could hardly contain himself when he described an event in which he saw a shaman offer a chalice filled with Pepsi to a very old woman who proceeded to burp loudly enough to make a frat boy blush. Apparently, the louder and more powerful the burp, the more evil spirit is released. Heaven knows what power may lie beneath us. While I have some reservations about their means to an end, the fact that these folks acknowledge that within us there are some things that need to be expelled puts them one step ahead. Even if our shadows are, according to Jung, 90 percent gold (a gross overestimate), that still leaves 10 percent bullshit (more than enough to taint my jewelry!).

Once, on a snorkeling trip in the abundant, clear Caribbean waters near Cozumel, I managed to miss most of the marine life (what fish?) because, like all the other single gringos on the boat, I was mesmerized by a beautiful young woman from Colombia who was wearing a thong and swimming right in front of me. In Mexico, the line between sporting events and social events is blurred if not removed, so each reef visit was followed by two tequila shots. (Please do not try this at home.) By the third reef, despite the communication barrier (she spoke no English and my Spanish is such that I have a lot to learn from the Taco Bell Chihuahua), and despite the fact that her mother was sitting right next to her scowling at me, I was flirting so hard I lost a flipper. In reality, I was simply doing a lot of staring and mumbling the eloquent, articulate, romantic words *muy bonita* over and over. I think she really liked me too. She kept saying something about *loco* which I believe translated as "I love you, and I want to have your children." My Spanish began to improve after the tequila, and in an attempt to win the mother's affection, I explained that I am a *padre de la iglesia* (a priest of the church). The mother swelled up like a pufferfish and yelled, "*Sí, un padre! Un padre de los bambinos, todos los bambinos!*" Then she shook her finger in my face, pointing right at me and said, "*El Diablo! Eres El Diablo!*" In case you are unclear about the translation, let's just say that she thought I worked for the other guy. She was confusing me with the competition. For the rest of the trip, and even to this day, to some I am still affectionately known as *El Diablo*.

Call me shallow. Call me sinful. Call me downright disgusting. Quite frankly I resemble those remarks. But so do you, in your own way. There's a little *diablo* in every one of us. Whether we choose to ignore it, corner it, or whip its ass, a good start is to fess up and call it what it is: wrong. And first to look inward before we look outward. While obsessing about the speck-sized evil in others, we ignore the log-sized evil in ourselves. This obliviousness is at our own peril—and may eventually be dangerous for the greater world.

And be careful of overzealous, misguided attempts to confront what may or may not be the real thing. Too many times the easy targets of our wrath are merely projections of our own shortcomings. Whether right or wrong, we tend to pick on and label that which is not us, is unlike us, and does not serve our own needs and interests. Such false attempts to vilify are greater evils in themselves. For example, in recent years a number of so-called Christian organizations have worked themselves into a frenzy and declared moral war on the following black holes of depravity: Mickey Mouse, Barney the Dinosaur, and Tinky Winky the Teletubby. I am sure that we all sleep better knowing someone is taking on these mascots of immorality. Please! These furry television creatures are not the enemy. The enemy lurks in even more improbable places: our churches, our homes, our hearts.

In Mrs. Brackett's eleventh-grade geometry class (I am sure it is mere coincidence that Mrs. Brackett and geometry come to mind in the context of evil), I once waged war against a wasp. I am not certain how the wasp was able to enter Mrs. Brackett's eleventh-grade geometry class, nor what the wasp's motive could possibly have been, but there he was. Intentionally present or not, justifiably pissed or not, the wasp was terrorizing the entire class, soliciting squeals of horror from several of the girls and nervous groans from a few of the guys. Zipping past my theorem-laden head, the wasp alighted on an adjacent window. Not having time to calculate the precise angle of my arm or posit a proof in defense of the wasp's position, I grabbed my geometry notebook, at last putting it to practical use, and swatted the dangerous intruder. My linear weapon made contact with the solid surface, sending the shattered, unclassified geometric patterns of glass shards straight toward the horizontal plane of the courtyard lawn. The wasp, seizing its freedom, flew directly across campus, forming in flight a perfect trapezoid before landing in Calculus 101—just to spite me, I'm sure.

Mrs. Brackett was not amused and thrust a one-way ticket to the principal's office in my direction, bellowing that my overt act of vandalism would not go unpunished. She perceived my intervention to be highly inappropriate, if not incorrigible, while my intent was to engage in a heroic act of self-defense and protect my classmates from certain harm. My father and the assistant principal debated my motives for several days. My father proudly pointed out that "if more people took action like my son did, the world sure would be a better place," neglecting to mention the potentially positive economic impact on the glass industry. Eventually they compromised, with me paying half and the school paying the other half to repair the window. The wasp paid nothing.

Was my behavior a brave and beautiful move or a thoughtless, misdirected, if not slightly malicious maneuver? Was I simply projecting my own bad boy onto the innocent wasp? Was my subconscious motive to disrupt what I perceived to be a pointless exercise, to challenge authority, and attract the attention of the hottie two desks ahead of me? Wasn't the wasp merely behaving as wasps are genetically programmed to act, exhibiting nothing more harmful than the natural inclination of such a species?

Hell if I know. The complexities of creation and human behavior continue to elude me. I do know that my motives are rarely pure, a wasp's stinger in my neck is hardly beneficial for humanity or for the wasp, and sometimes our natural inclinations are just plain wrong. My desire to sting you or to screw you may be perfectly normal or even ethically justifiable, but such legitimizers don't make it right. I may have the potential to soar like an eagle, but I am just as capable of spraying like a skunk. For every flower I pollinate, there is another that I trample. There's a fine line between a tender kiss and a painful bite, and I am quite capable of both.

In the difficult desert of far West Texas they call the Despoblado, the depopulated land, near the tiny town of Marfa, artist Donald Judd has created a unique art compound called Chinati, named for the mountains in the distance. At the end of a gravel road, a young intern pointed toward Claes Oldenburg's masterpiece, *Monument to the Last Horse*. It is a massive horseshoe, a protector of hooves, which changes directions with the wind. Along the way, the young artist stated the ultimate irony for such contextual art. "Out here," she said, "dust is our worst enemy." An interesting observation to be made in the desert.

And so it is. Out there. And in here. Dust may be our best friend. And our own worst enemy. Remember that reality the next time you bathe. That we are dust, and to dust we shall all return.

In the meantime, on our respective journeys, should we, like Sam, come face-to-face with something vaguely reminiscent of angels, do not delay. Do not be deceived.

Run.

Like the devil.

CHAPTER 13

∙∙∙∙∙∙∙∙∙∙∙

Be Not Afraid

Perfect love casts out fear.
1 JOHN 4:18

Sam, like my mother used to say about my ex-wife, ain't afraid of nothin'! Sam is not frightened by any number of things which could be cause for alarm: the night, nuclear holocaust, oncoming traffic, religious programming on television, crime, failure, bioterrorism, the diminishing ozone layer, bigger beasts than he, or the far-right wing of the Republican Party. He does get annoyed and tries to avoid certain mean-spirited, territorial dogs in the neighborhood, and he sometimes exhibits a playful reverence for the vacuum cleaner, steering clear of its sweeping path. But there is only one item on life's agenda of which Sam is deathly afraid, which makes his paws quake and sends him scurrying for protection. I refer, of course, to the terrifying, intimidating, bloodcurdling *ironing board*!

Simply removing the ignoble ironing board from the closet pushes Sam's panic button into overdrive. Faster than you can say "no starch," Sam begins racing around the apartment, frantically searching for a bomb shelter, a doghouse, or even a school desk under which to duck and cover. Sam's obsessive retreat takes him under the bed, into the bathroom, between my legs—anywhere he might find a haven from the malevolent monster. Cowering in a corner is mere child's play compared to Sam's dizzying pinball maneuvers—anything to protect and preserve his own hide from Boardzilla.

If you actually dare to open and set up the grotesque nightmare on legs, Sam will flee to the closest human and attach himself tighter than a topless dancer to a rock star. He will press up against you so close you couldn't squeeze a cent, much less a dollar, between the two of you. In the time it takes to iron a sleeve, the king of the terriers is reduced to a Velcro appendage and remains in that state until the garments have been pressed and the danger has been tucked back into its hallway tomb.

Perhaps Sam's unfounded fears have something to do with Rachel's own doubts about the ironing apparatus. I once noticed a burn on the upper portion of Rachel's arm and asked what had happened.

She replied sheepishly, "Oh, that happened while I was ironing a shirt," and tried to change the subject.

"How in the world did a hot iron scorch you above the elbow?" I wondered. "Were you doing weightlifting curls with it?"

"No," she admitted, "but I was in a hurry, so I ironed the shirt while wearing it."

That's one way to get around the board.

Apparently, her aversion to such household chores and their accompanying accoutrements was learned at a very young age. Her family is fond of telling the story of a conversation Rachel had with her grandmother in Tennessee when she was around four years old. The grandmother, trying to instill some sense of traditional feminine obligation and southern family responsibility in the impressionable young girl, stated, "Now Rachel, I'm sure you help your mother out with work around the house, don't you?" to which Rachel responded, "Well, I would, Granny, but so far I just haven't found any work that I like." Like Sam, Rachel would prefer a trip to the dry cleaners to a wrestling match with the ironing board.

I, on the other hand, am completely unintimidated in the presence of ironing boards. Exhibiting an uncommon courage in the face of such domestic challenges, I simply arm myself with a telephone and call the maid. That is not to say that I am phobia-free. For I am quite afraid of certain wild beasts, the kind that lurk far beyond the bedroom closet.

I suppose my cowardice toward the wild can be traced to my childhood. My country cousins, Chuck and Calvin, would sometimes chase me around the pasture with creepy-looking crawfish they had pulled out of the ground. As a city boy, I am still not afraid of the seediest parts of downtown after dark, but those squirming mudbugs have managed to embed themselves in my psyche to this very day. The only food to which I am allergic on the entire planet? Crawfish. And I do love that Creole cooking!

Then there was the annual summer vacation with Rosemary and Hank Bartos to New Braunfels, a fun little German town on the edge of the Texas Hill Country, a small slice of heaven on earth for a child. All of us kids would float and swim and dive all day long in the clear, cool waters of the Comal River, breaking just long enough to play barefoot in the grass of the gentle, sloping banks or on the big common lawn between the cottages. I wore my swimsuit twenty-four hours a day and didn't unpack my shoes until we headed home.

That is, until my bare foot stepped on an unseen asp and he stung the naïveté right out of me. I had never even heard of an asp before that unpleasant encounter. Hank's joke that an asp was an insect with a big butt and a lisp did not make the pain go away. I was on the disabled list and out of the lineup for the duration of that vacation.

Shortly after the great asp uprising, I came to discover that there is no fortress impenetrable by any such fierce wild beast. One late night, in the safe confines of our home, my mother let out a bizarre yelp from the kitchen. "Oh, Bill," she screamed at my father, "I've been stung!" and began to cry. A scorpion had invaded our family territory and had sunk his stinger into my mom. My father came racing into the room waving a leather house shoe and pounded the tail right off of the uninvited pest. As I lay on my bed trying to sleep later that night, I wondered, *Is my own house not safe?* The answer, I knew, was no.

Even as an adult, I have had an occasional run-in with the least of these creatures. I have a favorite monastery in California to which I retreat for spiritual refreshment. Its setting is inspired. It sits atop a bluff in the mountains, overlooking Santa Barbara. On a clear day, you can see the Pacific Ocean. The coffee is freshly ground and blended by the monks, and they bake bread every morning. There are three well-stocked libraries with comfortable couches. There is a Mexican chef. California girls dwell just at the base of the mountain. I love to suffer for Jesus there.

Beyond the back gates is a vast wilderness preserve called Rattlesnake Canyon. The monks insist that its name is derived from the winding, snakelike shape of the area.

I believed them, until my first trek to the top was halted halfway up as a five-foot rattler slithered across the trail just ahead of me. I felt a sudden urge to retreat to the library below and read the entire book of Ecclesiastes. I still hike that canyon, but I now spend much more time down at the beach. And I watch my step wherever I go.

Bears remain my beast of choice—to avoid, that is. One year my buddy Jack and I set off for a true wilderness experience in early spring among the Collegiate Peaks near Leadville, Colorado. As usual, Thoreau-like in our simplicity, we took with us only a couple of books, two shotguns, a large cooler of red meat, and a case of the Belgian monks' finest (beer, that is). Mountain men with theological degrees, we imagined ourselves on our way to Walden in a four-wheel-drive, all-terrain vehicle.

We bounced our way up the mountain road and pitched our tent in an idyllic spot near a refreshing, snow-cold stream. We set up camp, built a fire, cooked our steaks, toasted the stars with our stream-chilled beverages, and settled in for an evening of stimulating discussion. I figured we would make our annual foray into our two favorite mystifying topics: religion and women. Not at the same time, of course, and not in that order.

Instead, Jack wanted to talk about bears. Especially how cantankerous bears can be after hibernating all winter; how bears can smell a camper a mile off; how bears would probably follow a stream down from the top of a mountain; how smart bears are; what strong claws, big teeth, and voracious appetites bears have; how bears are attracted to fires, steaks, beer, priests, and four-wheel-drive vehicles. And how Jack had a friend who knew a neighbor who had heard of an acquaintance who had been attacked by a bear last year. Then he proceeded to share his favorite Far Side comic in which a bunch of bears surround popular psychologist John Bradshaw. "He says we should get in touch with our inner cub," one bear says. Another offers, "I say, let's eat him."

It was more than I could bear.

Being the brave trooper that I am, I volunteered to sacrifice the outdoor experience and sleep in the car. After all, someone needed to guard our transportation throughout the night. If a bear did come down and drive off in our car, we would really be in trouble. "Excellent point, Bill," Jack noted as we said goodnight.

I took a little teasing from Jack after that night in the car. If the truth be told, however, Jack slept with a shotgun in his tent the whole trip. The following year he bought a travel trailer.

Our fears manifest themselves in multiple forms. I have a good friend who is not afraid of ironing boards or bears but does fear the dark. She sleeps with a nightlight on and never goes anywhere without a flashlight. I happen to like the night, but after my first real encounter with it, I wasn't so sure.

I attempted that adolescent rite of passage whereby the challenge is to escape from your home in the middle of the night. You walk over to your girlfriend's house, wake and annoy her for a while, then return to your bed before sunrise, all without eliciting even a hint of suspicion from either of your soundly sleeping parents.

The first (and last) time I tried this feat, I was in the seventh grade. I had no doubt that I could handle anything the night could dish out. As the clock struck two (a.m.), I clumsily mangled my way out of my bedroom window, flattened a hedge my father was particularly proud of, and strutted down the dark streets to Gail Pender's house several blocks away. After I pelted her second-story bedroom window with flower bed bark, she awakened and informed me she was really glad to see me at such an ungodly hour, and now I should leave.

Feeling somewhat deflated, but no less triumphant over his *exploit de espionage*, the young Billy Bond headed home. I was only a few doors down when I encountered the ultimate horror. Without warning, I heard a mighty roar. In the blink of an eye, what seemed like a thousand flashing lights raced up the trees, eerily illuminating the entire neighborhood. There was no place to hide. My heart rate, for the first time during my adolescence, began to exceed my libido, and I hightailed it for home. But as I turned the corner, the flashing street fighter with monster wheels started after me, with giant puffs of noxious smoke billowing from its underbelly. There was no escape.

I was certain that either the Martians had just landed in Candlelight Plaza or the Lord had returned to judge the quick and the dead, and to atone for my sin, I would quickly be dead. I froze in my tracks as the mutant Hummer hissed and spewed its venomous mist right toward me. As the danger passed, I paused for a moment to catch my breath and then ran all the way home, trampling the hedge as I leapt right through the window and into my bed.

The next day I realized that, the night before, the Harris County Mosquito Control District had sprayed me along with rest of the neighborhood for mosquitoes. While flying insects left me untouched for months afterward, it would be years before I would leave my house in the middle of the night again.

Our fears sometimes paralyze us from the soul on up and drive us to make some pretty meaningless, if not destructive, choices. Most of us, like Sam, run from our fears: hiding in the security of relationships with people we don't really like or want to be near, pursuing addictive and obsessive behaviors which numb the pain and temporarily take our minds off the threatening terrors, fleeing from the depressing dark night of the soul which may in fact harbor our salvation. We often follow the herd toward blatant materialism, arming ourselves with accumulations we don't really want or need at the expense of those who go without. As Lily Tomlin once said, "Even if we win the rat race, we're still rats." And even if we run from the danger, chances are it will still be there when we return.

The objects of our apprehension may or may not be justified, but they cannot be denied. No one is immune from the fear factor. Even Jesus, upon entering the Judean wilderness all by himself just after his baptism, experienced a most terrifying forty days. The scripture says that Jesus was tempted by Satan (it doesn't get more scary than that), and was with the wild beasts (none of which were tame; all of which were hungry). But then, almost in passing, the evangelist notes, "and the angels waited on him." I doubt the passage means that they took his order from a menu or catered to his concierge requests, but somehow the angels were there, possibly lurking in the background, maybe just outside his field of vision, perhaps unseen, unheard, unrecognized. Yet they saw him through the whole ordeal, to the very end. They waited on him and with him until it was all over. They did not desert him. They did not flee. They did not pass judgment on his fears as silly and unfounded. They walked with him through the wilderness to the other side.

I believe that God often walks with us and waits on us in such hidden ways—unseen, unheard, unrecognized—until we realize that the torment is over, the danger is passed, and we are still breathing. Wherever beasts dwell or demons lurk, angels abound, seeking to see us through to the other side. Whatever crippling fear threatens to undo us, perfect love casts it out and puts us back together. Whenever we are forced to face an unknown enemy, we do not go it alone.

But, I'll admit, there are some pretty scary things always out there. Asps lurking in the grass. Snakes hiding in the canyons. Crawfish buried in the pasture. Bears foraging in the forest. Scorpions prowling in the kitchen cupboard. Insect nightstalkers, sneaking around our own neighborhoods. Ironing boards plotting in the hall closet.

Sam and I are still learning to be not afraid. We are learning to trust the Good Shepherd, to walk through the valley of the shadow of death and to fear no evil. We are recognizing that the Shepherd's rod and staff can provide great comfort, and that even if we can't see them, the angels are on our side. Meanwhile, there's nothing wrong with holding on to each other and reminding ourselves of a powerful truth: the dry cleaners is just around the corner.

CHAPTER 14

....

Fishy Stories

When Jesus had finished speaking, he said to Simon, "Put out into the deep water and let down your nets for a catch." Simon answered, "Master, we have worked all night long but have caught nothing. Nevertheless, if you say so, I will let down the nets."
LUKE 5:4–5

It has been said that fishing is an activity with a worm on one end and a fool on the other. I wholeheartedly disagree. It is far more likely that there is an artificial lure on the end opposite the fool. It is true, however, that the fool always occupies the end of the rod closest to the reel, but in fishing, as in life, that's not such a bad place to be.

When someone engages in a completely ridiculous activity or does something unquestionably foolish, I am often puzzled by the pejorative use of the phrase, "He has really gone off the deep end," to describe the situation. It seems to me that the deep end is quite preferable to the shallow end. The deep end allows for much more freedom of movement. The possibility of finding sunken treasure dramatically increases there, and diving is permitted. In the deep end, we can be much more creative with our belly flops. Besides, the farther you go from the shore, the more interesting and complex the aquatic life becomes. I'm not really certain what the attraction of the shallow end might be, but there seem to be a large number of people who prefer to stay there. All I know is, the deeper the water, the bigger the fish.

I have read in recent years that the Comal River in New Braunfels, Texas, is the shortest river in North America. In my five-year-old mind, it seemed as long as the Mississippi. I caught my first fish from its waters while on vacation with my surrogate parents, Rosemary and Hank Bartos. Rosemary and I would rise before the sun, pack our cane poles, bag of minnows, tackle box, and cups of coffee (heavy on the cream and sugar for me) and make the arduous early morning trek down the steep embankment from our cottage to the riverbank. I was such a big boy, practically a man I thought, to get up so early, drink such a strong beverage, bait my own hook, and reel in a whopper suitable for mounting.

As an adult, I went back to the Comal and realized that the terrain was just a gentle slope, and one could almost toss a trout into the river from the cabin's deck. We were that close to the water. The small perch I had caught, barely the size of a five-year-old's fist, should have been thrown back according to the law. And while we're being truthful and adultlike, I'll admit I actually didn't bait my own hook until the dawn of adolescence. Rosemary did it for me all those years. Even today, I prefer deep-sea fishing simply because you don't have to get anywhere near the bait.

Back then that tiny bob of the cork sent a shiver of excitement down my spine I had not experienced since the first time the ice cream man drove down our street. My overzealous yank of the cane pole nearly hooked the lip right off my poor fish's face. For thirty years my mother kept the postcard I sent home that read simply, "I caught two."

Over the years, my interest in fishing waned considerably. There were several unfruitful attempts on Oyster Creek with my cousin Dude using crickets as bait. I actually fished with a baitless hook, not wanting to admit that I wasn't about to chase down and capture a cricket with my bare hands. Besides, Dude was no more successful using an actual insect.

There were some bright spots such as the three-pound redfish I caught in Galveston Bay and a few flounder along the Texas coast, all with Rosemary and Hank, this time in their boat. But the remaining memories of those trips have more to do with sunburns, shrimp creole, and the smell of vinegar than with fishing.

My brother and I would occasionally accompany my father in the middle of the night to the Freeport jetties or some lighted fishing pier on the Gulf. I remember spending most of my time untangling fishing line, getting my hook caught on rocks, and eating all the sandwiches before sunrise. I typically landed a worthless three-ounce hardhead and spent way too much time trying to figure out how to detach this sharp-whiskered cat from the hook without getting myself sliced. After several years of such pointless sleep deprivation, my brother took up surfing, while I scoured the beach for shells and later for bikinis. Dad kept on fishing.

Years later, on a trip to Cozumel, my buddy Michael Soper insisted we go deep-sea fishing. "People come here from all over the world to catch dorado," he said, guaranteeing I would hook one. After painfully paying the equivalent of twelve perfectly good cases of Corona that could've been consumed on a lounge chair under a beach umbrella, we boarded Captain Pablo's boat with two young honeymooners from Oklahoma. Perhaps it was the ungodly hour of the morning. Perhaps it was the intense August heat. Perhaps it was the diesel fumes that permeated the entire vessel. Or it could have been the twelve-foot swells we encountered. I suppose it may have been the fact that the night before I had ingested five margaritas, four shots of tequila, three beers, two lime liquados, and a large taco platter, topped off by a fine Cuban cigar and a fistful of aspirin. Whatever it was, my stomach was churning like a butter factory. After puking from the backside of the boat all the way to Playa del Carmen, I apologized to the honeymooners. Michael thoughtfully brought me a cool, refreshing beer to settle my stomach. Just what I needed. Unfortunately, it was the only beverage the captain had cooled for the journey. To make matters worse, since we had caught no fish whatsoever, Michael paid the captain an additional fifty bucks for an additional hour of misery.

Just before we got back to shore, however, I caught a 10-pound dorado (that's mahi mahi on your seafood platter). I suddenly felt much better. Pictures don't lie. "Hold the fish way out in front of you," Michael instructed. "It'll make it look bigger than it really is." Besides, that way the fish could obscure some of the taco platter remnants covering my T-shirt.

By the time we disembarked, the captain had filleted our little friend, I had regained my appetite, and the world had stopped floating. We walked into the first restaurant we saw and asked the chef to work his magic on our fresh catch. He prepared our two-hundred-dollar fish (not that I'm bitter) five tasty ways and we enjoyed one of the best meals of all time. In the process we made new friends by sharing our catch with neighboring diners.

So the next summer Michael had to promise me only that I would catch a billfish, which would somehow help me land the Latin girl of my dreams, to entice me into another deep-sea outing to the rich waters off the Costa Rican coast. I did not catch a billfish or land a Latina, for that matter, but that day still earned a prime spot on the highlight reel of my life. Like Moses at the Red Sea, our rods seemed to part the Pacific waters wherever we cast. Almost immediately, I caught a 40-pound dorado that made my Cozumel catch look like a guppy. Shortly thereafter, Michael caught a 39-pound dorado, a nice fish to be sure, just not as big as mine. The true fireworks came later when I hooked a 120-pound yellowfin tuna. It took every ounce of strength I could muster to land this guy. I nearly rubbed the skin off my finger, right down to the bone, as Charlie's tough cousin Vinny fought valiantly for almost an hour and a half. Michael, too, caught his dream catch, a massive sailfish that had sporadically pierced the open waters with acrobatic leaps toward the sky. After a quick photo, we released the beautiful but endangered creature back into his deep blue home. But not before he weighed in at 119 pounds. A rough guesstimate to be sure, but probably quite accurate. Certainly a very large fish, of which Michael should be proud, just not as large as my tuna. Not nearly as large.

Our captain, Jesse Fornetti, a fun-loving, fully baked, half-cocked transplant from New York, tried to coax us into an extended stay at the rustic hotel he called home with the promise of pot in every pot and the specially priced services of some teenaged Nicaraguan girls. "I'm a local. I can get you a good deal," he claimed. We graciously declined, but not before enjoying a feast of fresh ahi with Jesse, most of the hotel staff, and other various poolside acquaintances.

The thrill of sharing our sea bounty with strangers for the next leg of our journey up the Pacific Coast was almost as gratifying as pulling our prizes out of the water. Like the biblical feeding of the five thousand, our ice chest of two fish (technically only a small portion of the dorado and tuna) endeared us to the multitudes, all manner and sort of hungry traveler along the way. We made up for my previous tainting of postnuptial bliss by surprising a just-married couple with a honeymoon gift of fresh tuna steaks and dorado fillets. We savored a special six-course meal with an Italian chef at a nice resort, shared deep-fried fish chunks from a paper bag with fellow ferry passengers, and devoured a generous portion of Central American–style cuisine under a thatched beach hut in the middle of a thunderstorm with a guitar-strumming troubadour by candlelight. He reciprocated by allowing us a few puffs on a cigar he'd been saving for just such a special occasion.

I began to understand how the fishermen among Jesus' disciples must have felt as they set out simply to lower their nets and ended up catching a bunch of folks they hadn't even known before. Their priority became people, and their willingness to share became the bait that brought them in. A little fillet, when blessed, broken, and given, can go a long way. That which is finally savored is not what's mounted on the wall, but what's shared along the way.

My father fished to the very end, despite the obstacles and adversities he faced. After major surgery to remove a portion of his esophagus and stomach, numerous rounds of radiation and chemotherapy, and the loss of about fifty pounds and his once-hearty appetite, my dad received the sobering news that the cancer had spread to his liver. The oncologist indicated that a major new regime of chemotherapy should commence quite soon. My father asked one simple question of the doctor, "Will this treatment interfere with my fishing trip the first week in May?"

Dad made sure it would not interfere by wrapping up the first infusion on a Monday morning, jumping into his previously packed Explorer, and driving straight to the Piney Woods of East Texas to fish for a few days with his brother Jake. I had fond memories of Uncle Jake from childhood. I couldn't quite pronounce his name as a toddler and started calling him "Cupcake." After I finally mastered the word "uncle," it was too late to alter such a delicious name and instead he became Uncle Cupcake. Uncle Cupcake took me to see Don Drysdale and Sandy Koufax pitch in the Astrodome, shortly after its opening as the world's first domed stadium. To see a legend pitch in such a modern-day marvel was more than my little boy's mind could imagine. He bought me peanuts and a Coke, and when the Astros hit a home run, we even got to see the cowboy lasso the steer on the exploding, larger-than-life, one-of-a-kind scoreboard.

But the significance of my early baseball memory with Cupcake falls just short of the warning track compared to my father's final fishing memory with him. My dad called me upon his return from the fishing trip, a most unusual occurrence, so I knew something was up. He said nothing about his cancerous condition, but blurted out with the excited enthusiasm of a five-year-old, "I've caught a fifty-five-pound catfish! That's the biggest fish I ever caught in my whole life! Jake caught a thirty-two-pounder, but mine was bigger!"

My father, as far as I knew, had never been deep-sea fishing and so had to forego the really big guys. I am sure he would have considered such an excursion an overpriced luxury he could not afford. But he fished passionately his entire life, and always close to home—by the Brazos River, on the green lakes of East Texas, all along the Texas coast. In the twilight of his life, he had finally caught the big one, the one that had eluded him all those years. He carried a Polaroid of that fish in his wallet until he could no longer carry a wallet. It was the only photograph that ever took billfold precedence over the grandkids' school pictures.

We keep fishing for the same reason we keep going back to Las Vegas. One of these days, we're gonna reel in the big one. So we bait our hooks with overbudget bait and cast a line as far out as our fleeting strength will allow. As it sinks into deep waters we do not know and cannot see, we patiently wait for what might surface, knowing that the big one usually gets away. And even if it doesn't, there is always a bigger one still out there. Faith keeps fishing: taking one last pull on the slot machine before boarding the plane, making one last phone call to the girl who already said, "I'd rather date a sea slug," pleading one last prayer before one last breath. It casts one last time though we've come up empty all day long. It is the faithful "nevertheless" that lets down the net yet again.

CHAPTER 15

. . . .

A Lighter Shade of Tail

Yonder is the sea. . . . And there is that Leviathan that you made for the sport of it.
PSALM 104:25A, 26

Sam has quite a sense of humor, which is one reason that I believe he is such a spiritual being. A sort of doggai lama, Sam is. For the Creator is also quite the cosmic comedian.

While biblical scholars debate the identity of the Leviathan, the psalmist is clear that God made this big boy of the sea just for fun. Biblical scholars, many of whom abandoned their senses of humor at the seminary steps, conjecture that Leviathan may have been a whale or a large fish. Some even go out on a limb to suggest a possible link to Nessie, the Loch Ness monster, or some sort of buoyant dinosaur out for a dip. Regardless of his genetic composition, I speculate that anyone named Leviathan had to be at least as entertaining as Liberace in Las Vegas. I could envision Leviathan (his stage name) arising from the dancing waters of his very own casino showroom, sporting green sequins for scales, wearing electric eels as fringe, surrounded by a bed of singing oyster showgirls. The ability to entertain does not necessarily correspond to the level of talent. Have you heard Wayne Newton lately?

In spite of Sam's inability to carry a tune, he is a highly effective entertainer and never ceases to make me laugh. Sam's sense of humor appears to be God-given, divinely inspired, and devoid of all ego. Even when I tell him, "Sam, we're not laughing *with* you, we're laughing *at* you," he continues to go on with the show.

Sam is funny enough in and of himself. His comedic appearance—a disheveled bouffant of hair, missing ears, and mischievous teddy-bear-gone-bad smirk—consistently provokes at least a smile. It's not uncommon, while Sam is riding shotgun in my truck, to see people stopped at traffic lights point at him and laugh out loud. If I park and make a quick pit stop at the convenience store or the cleaners, Sam immediately moves over to the driver's side and sits up straight, right behind the steering wheel. The ol' dog driving trick gets 'em every time, too. And even when we go out on walks through the neighborhood, oncoming pedestrians break into big grins the closer Sam gets. All he has to do is walk toward them.

Sam's stand-up routine, however, is a one-paw wonder. His overdone humor will not get him a time slot on Comedy Central anytime soon, but at least it's consistent. His sole joke, which he loves to play on you when he thinks you least suspect it, consists of Sam laying down on the floor and assuming the "Oh, never mind me, I've been asleep for hours" pose. "A pack of wild poodles could not disrupt me from my deep slumber," he convincingly suggests with his stone-cold pose. He will pretend to be sound asleep, dead to the world, oblivious to all, and will throw in a snore or two just to make sure you're sure. And then, when all is quiet on the canine front, just as you sneak past him, he suddenly springs to life, howling all the way up at the hilarious joke he's played, wagging his tail fast and furious, as if to say, "Ha! Surprised you!"

Okay, so it's not very sophisticated humor. He's a dog. You were expecting Chris Rock or George Carlin? Still, pretty comical for a canine, I'd say.

What makes this hairy little jokester even funnier is that he always gives himself away; his tail reveals the punch line long before it's delivered. If you watch him very closely you will see that not only does Sam keep one eyelid open just enough to squint and see where you're located; Mr. Sound Asleep's tail also consistently betrays him. He cannot contain the excitement of completing another Oscar-caliber performance and thumps the floor with his tail in anticipation of the big surprise. Despite his thespian somnolence, his wagging tail has a mind of its own and warns the innocent passerby of the prank in progress. Such Airedale antics never cease to amuse me. And although I feign surprise every time, the genuine amusement is never faked. As contrived as it may be, it really is funny!

Recently I was conducting an interview with an accomplished young journalism student for a part-time assistant's position. Her résumé was impressive, her education extensive, her poise quite polished. In the middle of the interview, just as we began to talk about spirituality and the writing process, Sam decided that the proceedings were getting far too serious, that the solemnity of the occasion did not warrant what he perceived to be stoic posturing on our parts. So, in an embarrassing effort to lighten things up a bit, Sam paraded between us, plopped down at the poor girl's feet, and began vigorously licking the carpet in her presence. "Stop that!" I immediately reprimanded Sam for his inappropriate and unsubtle behavior. "Sam has never licked the carpet before," I said apologetically. Sam then immediately flounced on his back and exposed himself without shame for both of us to see and began to perform almost acrobatic pelvic thrusts into the air, humping the atmosphere for no apparent reason. Thankfully, the young student found his terrier tomfoolery more charming than offensive, and she laughed right along with his attention-getting capers. She too had a sense of humor, and thus is not far from the Kingdom.

G. K. Chesterton once said, "The angels can fly for they take themselves lightly." We often find ourselves weighed down by nothing more than the gravity of our own attitudes. We are far too serious about ourselves and our spirituality and, more often than not, have turned religion and the spiritual quest into a burdensome chore, when humor, in fact, is the fuel in the furnace of the soul.

Not long ago I told a joke about Episcopalians to a room full of Episcopalians (such rooms are sometimes referred to as "country clubs"). It was the old joke about how many Episcopalians it takes to change a lightbulb. The answer, of course, is ten: one to replace it and nine to admire the beauty of the old, expired bulb. There is another version, of course: one to call the electrician and nine to mix the drinks. As with most good jokes, it is offensive only to those who need to be offended. As I told this joke, I kept my eye on one particular member of the group whose nickname was "Fishface." When I got to the punch line, for a fraction of a second he could not restrain himself, and a smile overtook his mullet-mouth. Catching himself in mid-smile, he literally drew his hand across his face and wiped the grin right off, immediately returning to his original puckered pickerel.

Where in the world did we get the idea that wretchedness and righteousness have anything to do with one another? That the less we laugh, the more holy we must be? That the longer the face, the stronger the case we can make for our own salvation?

W. H. Auden once observed, "It was generally the pleasure-haters who became unjust." The uptight are rarely as upright as they assume. Those who get the joke are those who get the joy—and generally those who make the world more enjoyable (and just) for all.

Each year I top my Christmas tree with a frog riding a sled. He is most unlike the beautiful, delicately lighted gold angel with curly blond hair that topped my parents' tree. Now she had class. Reverently rigid, with a frozen angelic expression, she piously pointed her glowing candles upward to the heavens.

My frog is another story. Dangling from above, a gangling presence on a sled not necessarily frog-friendly, he may seem out of place to some purists, eliciting gasps of surprise, ludicrous chuckles, or even titters of inappropriateness from holiday revelers. I have been questioned, criticized, and judged for placing this irreverent creature in such a hallowed spot. But there is something about his glittering rhinestone skin, his gaping bright red mouth, his bulging, mischievous eyes, and his spindly, sprawling green legs. They somehow elevate him above all the other ornaments.

The sled-handling frog is precariously perched on a limb near the top, looking as if he'll do a belly flop or an unplanned slalom at any moment onto the presents below. I have found him swimming in the stand of water below the tree trunk, and every year he manages to skydive at least once, usually taking a bell, a reindeer, or even a stained-glass ornament with him to the tree skirt below. But my Christmas frog is here to stay. He reminds me of the ultimate absurdity of the season, and his mode of transportation reminds me of the faith required to believe it. He makes me laugh, helping me get all the way from Advent to Epiphany, prodding me to pay attention to such frog flexibility, de-stressing me by stressing the age-old truth: when the going gets tough, the tough loosen up.

My Christmas Eve sermon sometimes reiterates this theme of the surprising, out of place, yet absurdly appropriate gift. One Christmas I bought my nephew Chris a "Mucous Man" and a "Snot Boy" from a local artist. These hilariously crafted clay figurines utilized the contents of a hot glue gun to represent discharges from the human sinus cavity. I knew my nephew with his twisted sense of humor would appreciate these two fine works of art, suitable for collecting.

That same year my father was being very picky and precise about the style of underwear he was to receive for Christmas. No boxers for dad. Nothing that came packaged in a tube, or appeared in exotic colors or patterned fabric. Traditional white cotton briefs only. And the briefs must have, for the love of the captain, a "kangaroo pouch." If the briefs did not have the requisite kangaroo pouch, he implied at every family gathering from Labor Day on, we may as well buy him a package of gold thongs or a bikini adorned with neon-colored bananas. We heard so much about the engineering brilliance and utilitarian design of this miracle of modern comfort, that we all rushed out and bought stock in Fruit of the Loom. For Christmas, my father received enough kangaroo pouches to house most of the Australian outback.

When I arrived at the kangaroo-pouch portion of my sermon (what my homiletics professor would call the "what the hell are you doing in that pulpit anyway?" or "I cannot believe you went there" section), just after the detailed descriptions of Mucous Man and Snot Boy, my eyes fell upon a very serious-looking, prim and proper, reserved, older woman sitting near the back of the church. I watched as her eyes dilated and inflated, her skin turned paler then Frosty the Vampire's, and her facial expression tightened toward a self-righteous crescendo. She looked as though, with Miss Manners pushing on one side and the Chief Pharisee shoving on the other, an invisible vise tightened around her head, giving it another spin with every tasteless homiletic metaphor I uttered. I believe it was one of the very few times my sermon literally nauseated someone. I cannot remember the point of my sermon, unless I was trying to prepare my listeners for the equally

Sam as a puppy, with ears.

Sam and Bill at the rectory, getting ready to greet guests at the annual Christmas party.

Sam as a puppy, peering through Rachel's hair.
Photo by Karen Dickey

Sam gives Rachel a kiss in the Baylor Street yard.
Photo by Karen Dickey

Facing page: Jack at his first Blessing of the Animals service at Trinity
Episcopal Church in Houston.

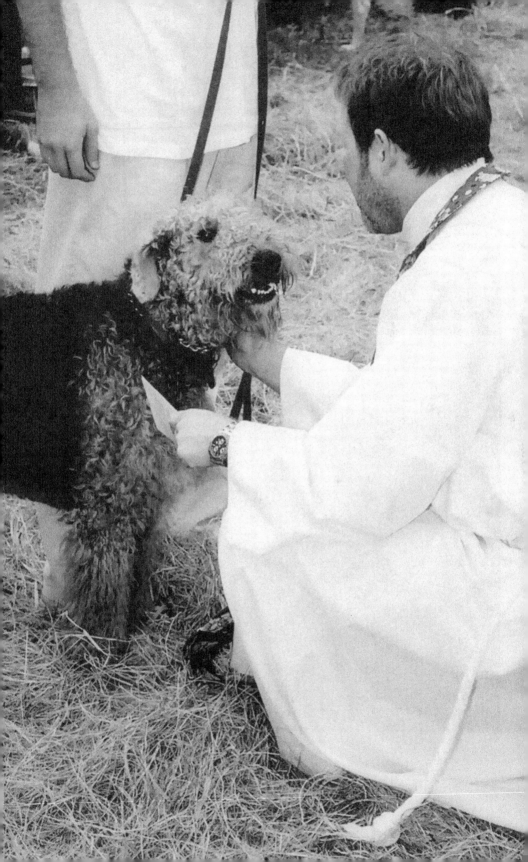

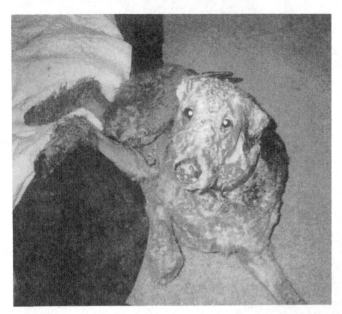

Sam, resting on a
futon, shortly after the
fire and when he was
finally able to lie down
again.

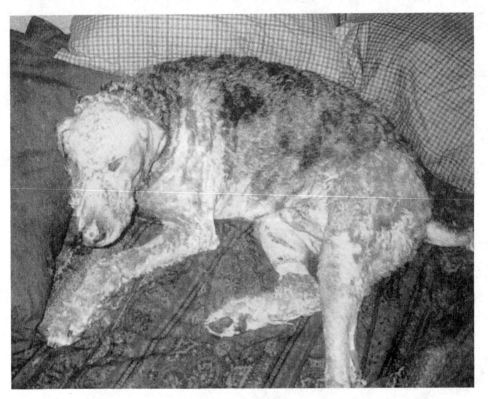

Rachel's neighbors on Baylor Street hung a "Sam Is Innocent" banner out the window one week after the fire, after the fire department labeled Sam an arsonist.
Photo by Karen Dickey

Sam's first post-fire outing, a get-well party thrown by neighbors. Sam eschewed the giant cookie with "Get Well Sam" written in frosting, choosing instead to stick his burned nose into homemade ice cream.
Photo by Karen Dickey

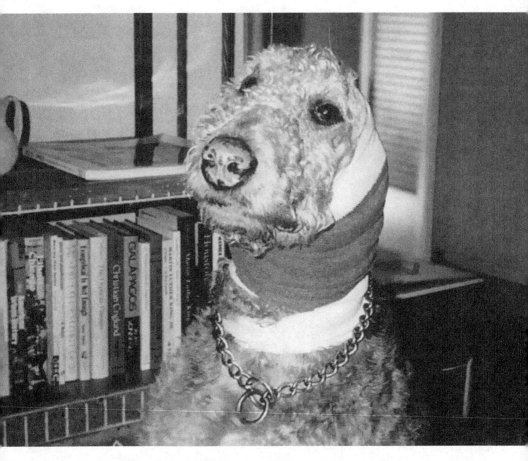

Sam sports his "Mother Teresa" look after the surgery in which his burned ears were amputated.

Jack and Sam on Jack's first day in the family in Austin, already wrestling.

Sam (left) and Jack (right) riding double-dog shotgun in Rachel's truck.
Photo by Karen Dickey

Jack, Bill, and Sam at the bay house.
Photo by Carol Barnwell

intimate, almost offensive, downright hilarious, unbelievable gift that is Christmas. So what if I got eggnog on my face? If the aesthetics of an overly runny nose or the powerful image of a grown man demanding a kangaroo pouch to protect his male marsupials can't get through to her, how will she ever understand the virgin birth or any other Christmas miracle?

The "I fail to see the humor in that" faction has been present in religious institutions since their inception. Near the Sea of Galilee, I walked through the ruins of an ancient structure that for centuries was a place of Christian worship. Interspersed in the well-preserved tile floor were some beautiful mosaics of pomegranates and ducks, symbols of the contextual reality for these worshipers by the sea. Their building committee, way back then, must have had quite a sense of humor to select pomegranates and ducks, respectively the funniest fruit and animal in that region, to adorn their floor. They could have picked dates and trout, for example, which would have been much less humorous, or even grapefruit and oxen, downright humorless options.

On the floor of this long-abandoned house of worship, the pomegranates remain, but the ducks have been obliterated. They were destroyed by a later group of Christians, among whom were some iconoclasts. The iconoclasts were, ironically, not very original in their thinking, and had heard or read somewhere that to be "faithful" (i.e., to agree with them), one should oppose any image of a living creature in a sacred space. In fact, this group was quite certain that nowhere in Scripture is the use of ducks authorized for worship.

These dour souls, probably just upset that their beloved prune lost out to the pomegranate, turned into duck-terminators for the Lord and set out to rid their sanctuary of the evil fowl. They succeeded—with one exception. Among the ruins, in an obscure corner of the tile floor, there is a single brave bird that withstood the wrath of the duck-haters. If you look very closely, you will notice there is a distinct smile across his bill. My fellow pilgrims and I nicknamed our surviving feathered friend "The Lone Danger." He is the ultimate antidote for the terminal seriousness that plagues so much of religion, a reminder that those who lose their sense of humor tend to lose their sense of direction, and that all of our modern-day mallard-beaters need to put down their mallets and go pet a duck. Or eat a pomegranate. Anything to get some perspective. Such intolerant warmongers remind me of the old Austin Lounge Lizards' song "Jesus Loves Me—But He Can't Stand You." Now that's funny.

One year, the St. James Pet Blessing on St. Francis Day made it into the local newspaper. That year a young girl named Krista, who didn't attend church very often, warmed my heart and enlarged my understanding of community by saying, "I'll be back next Sunday, and I'm bringing my grandmother's poodle." The church, I still tell people, should be a place where even a grandmother's poodle is welcomed. The day after the blessing, there was a large photo of me in the paper with arms outstretched over Ozzie and Harriet, the two pet turtles of a wonderful gay couple in my congregation. The clever caption read, "Bless me father, for I am a pet!"

A fundamentalist friend saw the photo and asked me incredulously, "How could you keep a straight face?" As if sacramental moments, or at least officially sanctioned religious events, had to be accompanied by a straight face. "I didn't," I replied. I laughed my way through most of the service.

Life's lasting blessings often do not come to us in the form of a straight face. Rather, we are blessed intensely by the surprised squeal, the gut-wrenching guffaw, the hearty belly-laugh, and the ludicrous, unpredictable, slapstick insanity that surrounds us. A religious service is precisely the place where we're let in on the Big Joke, where humor and grace permeate place, word, and act.

The final time Sam stopped by to see the preschoolers at St. James School was just such a sanctified moment. As Sam approached the playground area where the children were impatiently waiting, he began to suspect that he was the center of attention and strutted toward his shady makeshift throne near the tire swings. The children began to shout spontaneously, and in unison, "We want bow-wow! We want bow-wow! We want bow-wow!" The teacher and I would have probably described the scene by saying something dull like, "We want to provide an educational opportunity to observe canine behavior in an early childhood milieu." But the children said it better, as they often do. And the truth is I want bow-wow too. Don't you?

It was a magical moment. As the children approached Sam, they seemed to sense that they were standing on holy ground. They wanted desperately to pet him and to feed him goldfish crackers. But they also stood in awe of this eighty-two-pound creature, almost three times their size, with such big sharp teeth, and omnipresent wooly fur. So it was with great reverence that they approached, slowly, cautiously, some hiding behind classmates, extending their palms apprehensively, sweetly, goldfish in hand, giggling with delight as the cheese treats disappeared in a millisecond. The only evidence remaining was a thin coat of Sam slobber. They held up their hands in horror and exuberance, in bewilderment and enchantment, not knowing whether to wipe their hands off on their pant legs immediately or never to wash that hand again. And in that moment I was reminded that we come into the presence of the Holy with just such a desire, approaching the altar of God awkwardly, reverently, wanting so desperately to draw near to God, to touch God and to be touched by God, to taste the substance of the spirit, and yet respect the mystery of that moment.

We stand there with eyes open, arms outstretched, mouths agape, tiny gift in hand, offering mostly empty palms, open to receiving a kiss from above, open to experiencing the joy, humor, and gladness of the mysterious Presence.

Oohs and aahs. Squeals and shrieks. Mirth and merriment. The rasping of tiny fingers embedded in dog fur, scratching just above the heart. These are holy sounds.

CHAPTER 16

············

When Dogs Poop

In all things, God works for good.
ROMANS 8:28

I had been told that dogs were chick magnets. Apparently, Sam had the idea that such an attraction meant dropping the mother of all lodestones at an Easter Parade. So much for animal magnetism.

Sam and I were out for a leisurely stroll along the Town Lake trails one glorious spring morning. Suddenly, I spotted the goddess of all my dreams, a veritable Austin Aphrodite, walking right towards us with a gorgeous female collie by her side. They glistened. They glowed. They strutted, then strode ever closer, while Sam and I, drunk with desire, swaggered, then staggered our way right into each other and almost off the trail, mesmerized by these twin beauties. As Cupid's arrow began to pierce my heart, nature's call apparently began working its way through other parts of Sam's anatomy and he suddenly put on the brakes and searched for an emergency exit.

Oblivious to Sam's sense of urgency, I dragged him toward the dynamic duo, covertly cursing in disbelief that he would pick such a prime time to misbehave and refuse to heel. The lass and lassie of our ultimate fantasies were quickly approaching and Sam was fit to be leashed. What was this perfect girl going to think of such an incompetent loser, one who couldn't even keep his dog in step on the trail? So I yanked harder on Sam's chain and Sam yelped in dismay and ran around my legs and we tied ourselves together in a knot and nearly fell on top of each other. We looked for all the world like Laurel and Hardy with a lasso. Meanwhile, Sam pushed his nethermost regions as close to the grass as he could get and let her rip.

As Aphrodite approached, she exchanged her enchantress aura for a Venus de Annihilo pose, menacingly pointed with disgust to Sam's behind and his pile of projectiles and said accusingly, "I think *that* may be your problem."

Her collie held her nose up and away, and they paraded quickly past us like runway models at a livestock show. The mutts with no papers, the bewitched bunglers, could do nothing but come to an embarrassing halt. As Sam squatted on his less-than-royal throne, I wanted to ask him, "And what pound did you escape from?" But alas, sweet Venus had pinpointed our mutual problem, and with her diagnosis, she flushed all our fantasies away.

According to Sam, sometimes you just have to stop and poop on the roses. And such a recycling process is less of a problem and more of a possibility than we might initially imagine. Sure, it's a mess in the meantime, and the neighborhood garden club may reject your membership application. But just wait until those flowers bloom come spring. Fertilizer, eventually, makes all things bright and beautiful.

My father once had the entire neighborhood bourgeoisie up in arms over the fact that he had discovered a former grazing pasture on the outskirts of town and hauled over seven truckloads of manure-laden topsoil from it to spread on his lawn. The grass all but disappeared under the coal-colored dirt. Its country-fresh aroma permeated every neighbor's home. The subdivision's property values, no doubt, temporarily plummeted. But the smell eventually went away, and when the grass sprouted up through that rich mineral bed, it was greener than the neighbors' envy. Suddenly, cow compost was one hot commodity. The neighbors begged my father to reveal the location of the bovine bounty, but he just kept right on shoveling.

When I was a seminary student living in the Hyde Park neighborhood of the south side of Chicago, my fellow students and I would toss aside our lexicons and theological dictionaries for a lively game of touch football every Friday afternoon. It was the Presbyterians vs. the Lutherans. Although I was predestined to become an Episcopalian, I had temporarily chosen to side with the Calvinists. It was a tough choice, but academics and scotch won out over music and beer.

The site of these scrimmages was a neighborhood park that I'm sure bore the name of some war hero, generous benefactor, or community activist. To all of us, however, it was known simply as Dog Field. On these hallowed grounds, the various dogs of the neighborhood would meet, not to frolic, but to take care of business. Frolicking is frowned upon in such a stately scholastic setting. Everything is strictly business, even for pets.

You can imagine how exciting our football games became. We had to dodge more than mere defenders. Running a pass route was not unlike tiptoeing through a minefield, and soft landings were not to be desired. Spring football was even more risky, as the snow had just melted to reveal an entire field of formerly frozen treasures newly thawed and just ripe for the slipping.

Win or lose, we would conclude such rowdy camaraderie by drinking away our sorrows and our smells at Jimmy's Woodlawn Tap, rumored to be the pub of choice for the great theologian Paul Tillich. We would pontificate *ad nauseam* over our pitchers of

Old Style and platters of polish dogs, dissecting and assimilating the knowledge recently imparted in the classroom. But the real theology was done back at Dog Field, close to the earth, in each other's faces, and often flat on our own.

The library certainly had its wisdom to offer us, but life's ultimate lessons were taught in the grubby trenches where the reading meets the road. Life and learning happened among the dung, amidst the obstacles and surprises, the ankle sprains, back strains, and shoe stains, the down-and-dirty places far below the ivory towers.

Once, I remember eyeing a particular pooch near Dog Field just as I was about to go out for a pass. I had absolutely no sympathy for his plight and immediately labeled him the enemy of all that is beautiful and good (and clean). Now that I have a dog, it is amazing how my perspective on such things has changed. All grass is fair game as far as I'm concerned, and Dog Field is a most appropriate use of public space. Another lesson learned. Until you have dodged a few land mines that your progeny has produced, found yourself up to your ears in a quite familiar mess, or roamed the neighborhood on a cold, wet night at 3 a.m. with a dog who has diarrhea, you don't know the half of it. Tolerance and true understanding are for those who have been halfway to hell and back, or at least slipped on dog dirt while trying to score the winning touchdown in the Reformation Bowl.

Perhaps you have heard about an anemic, short-lived craze that swept across our land many years ago (during the seventies, I believe; need I say more?). I am referring to the so-called pet rock phenomenon. It was the year lots of people (including my grandmother) got away with giving very cheap Christmas presents. The idea was that a real pet can be a lot of trouble, an inconvenience, and eat away your life savings. Why not adopt a rock as a pet? A pet rock would never knock over a bowl of Gravy Train, send a vet bill into the stratosphere, or run away with a pack of no-good strays. A pet rock would never engage in embarrassing behavior when guests come to visit, slobber on your new Italian suit, or wake you up in the middle of the night to play ball.

The pet rock phenomenon, while ancient history among today's hipsters, is alive and well in the religious realm. For the spiritually constipated, pet-rock religion works just fine. It is cheap and easily available. We don't have to feed it or pay attention to it. It never keeps us awake at night, and is always right where we left it. It never goes anywhere, grows any way, or does anything. It simply takes up space, causing no problems whatsoever.

No, thank you! I want a religion with a little Easter in it—where earthquakes stir up some dust, where stones roll right towards us. I want a spirituality that is alive, kicking, and licking. I want to be delighted and disgusted, repelled and resurrected. I don't want to warm the bench. I want to run amidst the mud and muck. In other words, I want to be alive!

The truth is that the best things this life has to offer are messy: barbequed ribs, cheese enchiladas, chili, sex, peaches, pets, prayer, ice cream cones, the beach, gravy, candles, family, friendship, church, love. Life-making, like lovemaking, is rumpled and untidy. So go ahead and pour on the Tabasco, tie on the bib, and hose me down. I'd rather live now and shower later. Please, no more sterilized religion, sanitized for my protection. No more force-fed tofu spirituality that is good for me, but no good at all, that doesn't require a napkin or a bath. I want something with meat on the bone, that might crack a tooth or give me indigestion, that drips hot-blooded red on to my starched white shirt, that sticks between my teeth and withstands the assault of the world's most formidable toothpick, that stays with me long after I leave the table. Give me that real-life religion, the kind that makes the mess rather than cleans it up.

My hometown of Austin has the largest urban bat colony in North America. Most of these funny little flying mammals live under the Congress Avenue bridge that crosses the lake downtown, but several years back some of them took residence at St. James Church. Apparently there was a tiny hole in the skylight at the apex of our ceiling, where they entered and slept away their days directly above the altar. At night they'd exit to eat bugs and return before sunrise. We rarely saw our nocturnal friends, but they provided enough evidence of their presence. Each Sunday morning we would find they had deposited a small amount of guano on the Lord's Table. Our altar guild got quite steamed about such foul manners and demanded that we patch the hole immediately before the altar was subject to further desecration.

Eventually we found a few thousand dollars to repair the skylight, but not before a Maundy Thursday service in which these terrifying tykes frightened our parishioners with low-flying air raids all around the sanctuary just after dusk. What is a scary enough service, with Jesus' farewell meal with his loved ones, demonstrative humility in washing their feet, betrayal by a close friend, agony in the garden, and impending crucifixion, became even more frightening. The overt danger of being seen with such a shady character as Jesus was made painfully real, as parishioners literally hid their faces from view, some scattering in the darkness, a few even leaving before the service ended. The whole surreal scene was not unlike the disciples' desertion of Christ when well-laid plans spun out of control, and everything got scary that very night.

In medieval times many of the larger European cathedrals drilled small hidden openings in the ceiling on the day of the Pentecost. At the appropriate moment in the liturgy, live doves were released into the cathedral to symbolize the presence of the Holy Spirit. As the swooping, diving birds made their point, I can imagine all the ducking, dodging, even screaming, especially should a dislodged missile find its target among the congregation below. It must have been glorious chaos, and a mess to clean up—just what the Spirit does best.

I hope that we do not, for safety's sake, plug all of the openings in our lives. In keeping out bats, we just may keep out doves. In sweeping up all the dirt, we could be tossing aside some hallowed ground. Cleanliness is far from godliness, and hermetically sealed lives eventually suffocate in their own sterility. One can learn to play the game by getting down and dirty with the dogs now and then.

My mother's favorite story to tell about me as a young boy centered on my learning to "give thanks in *all* circumstances" as the Scripture says—pitfalls, pratfalls, and all. Shortly after I learned to ride a bike, feeling superhuman cruising on my new stingray, I would often try to jump one curb, hill, or automobile too many and wipe out on the concrete below. I raced home with bloodied knees and sullied pride. My mom would greet me every time with a bottle of Bactine, a comforting embrace, and a profound theological insight. She always said the same thing in the same soothing voice: "Let's just stop right now and thank God. It could've been much worse."

"Thank you, God," she prayed, "that Billy is not hurt seriously and is going to be okay."

This episode played itself out so often that one day, after a
particularly nasty fall with scraped hands, skinned knees, and
blood pouring down my shins, I flung open the front door and
beat her to the punch, running through the house screaming,
"Well, thank God for that! Thank God for that!"

She did not spray or pray that day. She was laughing too hard.
So much for spiritual enlightenment.

It would take a true B.S. in theology to assume that the bull
won't charge simply because we're vegetarians. Life is no latrine,
but even the right path, perhaps especially the right path, is
marked by unforeseen pit stops, unpleasant potty breaks, goddess-
es who don't get it, unmarked landmines, surprise dive bombers,
and repeatedly skinned knees. And that's really not such a problem after all. It is simply the beautiful, horrible, paradoxically
bearable truth. We're all in the fertilizer business.

I say, Amen.

Thank God for that!

CHAPTER 17

....

Elephant Walk

"Sunday school." Those two words are enough to turn 80
percent of all young believers into avowed atheists for the
rest of their lives. While I do not have quantifiable proof, I would
suggest that most cases of Attention Deficit Disorder, psycholog-
ical disturbance, acid reflux, acne, and impotence are the direct
result of sitting at the feet of one too many maladjusted Sunday
school teachers. Potty training and puberty are mere after-
thoughts compared to the elephantine challenge of surviving
Sunday school. Those who do so without the aid of medication,
residential treatment, or prison should graduate immediately to
sainthood.

I can only imagine the questions posed on the prospective Sunday school teacher application. Have you ever wondered what it would be like to torture small children? Do you find yourself having sadistic thoughts during the sermon each Sunday? Can you maintain a monotonous, humorless state for long periods of time? Can you bore an entire room of people simply by your presence? If you answered "yes" to any of the above questions, the children of the Rattle Trap Church of Christ need you! Who needs padded rooms or sedatives when you've got Sunday school?

At my childhood church we had some exceptionally qualified applicants. There was Larry, the butch, young military wannabe who hated hippies, flowers, and love. He refused to vote in the '64 presidential election because Goldwater was too liberal. He had a flattop haircut and always wore a tie. He assumed that every young boy between the ages of three and five wanted desperately to be manhandled, lifted high into the air by his suspenders, twirled around, and made fun of. He reserved his special fury for me when I would wear my red velvet jacket with matching red velvet shorts. "Here comes cute little Billy," he'd sing, in a vicious, pre-punk sort of way, raising me by the throat and "tickling" me with the force of a heavyweight champion. Perhaps I should have been choked for wearing the red velvet outfit, but I was under the age of accountability, so blame it on my mother.

Brother Fobbs had been teaching the fifth-grade boys since the Apostle Paul retired. He was a frightening, hunched-over man who sat in a corner and fished loose, unwrapped candy out of his pants pocket, placing it on the table before us as if it were some delectable prize. When we would refuse to partake on basic hygiene grounds, he would slam his cane against the nearest chair and yell, "Fine! Don't eat it!" He would then segue into a hissing biblical quotation on the wrath of God. I learned a lot about wrath in his class. There was much to be feared.

Then there was the syrupy sweet Mrs. Mylie, a true pedagogical dream. Her use of the filmstrip projector was mesmerizing. Her telling of Bible stories, illustrated by colorful characters stuck to a flannel board, was captivating. Her sandbox lessons, a noble attempt to re-create the Judean desert, were inspiring. Her Bible plays, in which we acted out historic encounters, were moving and realistic. Although I will never forgive her for assigning me the role of the man with leprosy, taping blobs of white construction paper to my face, earning howls of derision from developing sixth-grade girls whose opinions mattered more than God's at that tender age. Mrs. Mylie was serious, well-prepared, and pious, and she expected the same from her students. We received a star each week for attendance, punctuality, participation, memory verse, and bringing visitors. We could also get credit for attendance even if we attended another church on a given Sunday. However, it wasn't until she refused to give Bruce Briscoe a star because he had attended a Methodist church, and said, "We all know the Methodists are going to hell," that I realized just how sweet such narrow-minded intolerance could sound. "Nice" people can sometimes be the carriers of the most deadly diseases.

Of course, I am prone to exaggerate with the hyperbole of biblical prophets. Truly, I was blessed with several excellent Sunday school teachers who did instill within me some significant values and helped me to understand the goodness of creation and the love of God. My favorite was probably Mrs. Kindrick, my teacher when I was three years old. It was my first time in a real Sunday school class, having hung out in the nursery up to that time. My first day in her class was memorable, and neither of us has forgotten it.

My father was a young, well-respected churchman in his late thirties at the time. He had served as deacon for several years, and everyone in the church assumed he was well on his way to becoming an elder. One of the qualifications of an elder was to have a "godly family," and even at age three I seemed hell-bent on impeding his progress toward that goal.

As we arrived at church that morning and my father scooped me up from the backseat of the car and carried me toward my rendezvous with Mrs. Kindrick, I felt a significant level of anxiety, not knowing what to expect from real Sunday school and not understanding precisely how such preschool theology might be imparted. My dad reassured me and headed toward Room 3. But just ahead and outside the door of my new classroom, I spotted Travis Starr and his father engaged in an all-out brawl. Travis, for some reason, did not want to go into that room (*good God, what must they be doing in there?*), and was throwing a super-sized tantrum—screaming, crying, kicking, and biting. "I don't want to go," yelled

Travis. His father, who was not on the fast track to elderhood and thus not in need of a "godly family," caved in and carried Travis on down the hall, perhaps to the adult class, perhaps some place where there were donuts, maybe even home. All I knew was it must be a better place, maybe some place where there was a television and no one learned anything. Seeing Travis throw his fit, I thought to myself, *What an immature baby. I think I'll try that. If it worked for Travis, surely it will work for me!* As we arrived at the classroom door and Mrs. Kindrick greeted us, I proceeded to get in touch with my inner crybaby and began a most convincing performance. "I can't go in there!" I wailed. "No, please no! God no! Help me!" My father, the sensitive type, shoved me off on Mrs. Kindrick, barked, "You're goin'!" and left the room. Now I was really upset.

There were other students already in the class. Having been a seasoned nursery performer, I knew how this worked. If I could simply maintain my wailing long enough, one of them would start believing that the world was unsafe and we were all in dire, imminent danger and start crying. Before long I could have the whole room reduced to utter, ungodly chaos, mothers and fathers rushing back in to rescue their precious children, as I boasted from atop the teacher's desk, "I warned you what a terrible place this is!" Unfortunately, the louder I cried, the more the students, seated around a table with their hands politely folded, looked at me as if I had just peed in the sandbox. Not one budged, whimpered, or gave me the time of day.

Mrs. Kindrick was quite resourceful in calming future clergy down. All around the room, on all the walls, she had posted large, friendly pictures of various animals. Holding me in her arms, she approached each one happily. "Look, Billy, here is the lion. The lion wants you here." Moving on, she exclaimed, "Look, Billy, there's the aardvark. The aardvark wants you here." And next to it, "Look, Billy, there's the skunk, the skunk wants you here." I was starting to get the message. Round the room we went, acknowledging the animal kingdom's conspiracy. It seems the platypus, the zebra, the alligator, the ostrich, and the toad all wanted desperately for me to be in Sunday school. But her coup de grace came when she thrust me right up toward the big gray elephant and marveled, "Oh, Billy, lookie there, the elephant really wants you here."

Well, hell, I thought, Why didn't you just say that from the start? If all the animals, including the elephant, want me in here, I guess I'll just stay. I stopped crying, calmed down, and relinquished my role-play satisfied that Satan was not, in fact, the Sunday school superintendent, that I would not be ripped apart limb from limb, and that any place with a bunch of animals who liked me couldn't be all bad.

By the end of the class I was leading all of the toddlers around the room in the elephant walk, a sort of primitive preschool dance whereby we would lumber left and right with giant strides, all the while waving our forearm trunks in front of us, clearing the jungle with the force of baby bulldozers. "Billy, you sure can do that elephant walk," Mrs. Kindrick would shout from behind her desk, avoiding the massive stampede. That's all I needed to hear as I pounded the earth with my massive elephant feet, swaying with enough rhythm to make Balanchine proud, extending my trunk so far out I elicited gasps from the other elephants. "You call those trunks?" I derisively wondered as the King of the Pachyderms led the herd on the eternal safari.

At last I had found my true calling. Each Sunday I waited to hear those magical words from Mrs. Kindrick, words that got my heart pumping, my blood flowing, my imagination soaring: "Billy, would you lead us in the elephant walk?" I would mightily, yet gracefully, extend my trunk and begin to sway with the full force of a mass gospel choir. All roads now led to India. The hills of Galilee became the majestic Himalayas. The thickest jungle, Eden itself, became a mere inconvenience when I came charging through. And God help you if you got in my way. It became a singular pursuit, the real reason I was in church each Sunday (much like pursuing girls in my later years). "I'm sure Jesus did rise from the dead, Mrs. Kindrick. Now can we do the elephant walk? Yes, I know the names of the twelve apostles. Now what about the elephant walk? When Christ returns, what will he want to find us doing? The elephant walk, of course." I was perhaps the greatest elephant walker in the history of the three-year-old class.

Unfortunately, over the years, opportunities for free-spirited movement in Sunday school became not only limited, but frowned upon. There was the brief popularity of the vacation Bible school song, "I'm in the Lord's Army," but the accompanying movements were more of a march than a dance, militaristic and regimented, with no room for spontaneity or interpretation. By the time I was of age to formally shake my booty, dancing was mentioned among other cardinal sins such as mixed swimming, long hair, and voting for George McGovern. By the time I attended a conservative Christian college in West Texas, being found in a dance club, even while doing the elephant walk, was cause for expulsion. The most popular joke around campus was that the administration had revised the policy to disallow sex while standing up, as it might lead to dancing.

So, it is no wonder my dancing abilities waned. There were occasional bright spots, such as my ex-wife informing me that my dancing reminded her of the Rev. Al Green—sensually smooth with a hint of religious fervor. My confidence cratered, however, several years later when I found myself presiding over an African American congregation. After a particularly rowdy social function, a member confided, "We all decided you preach much better than you dance." Then there was the time I really cut loose on a dance floor in the Caribbean with my Latin girlfriend. While I could compliment her moves as quite spicy, she asked me as we returned to our table after getting down, "You *were* kidding, right?" I had been very serious.

By adulthood, I had completely forgotten about my early childhood prowess with the elephant walk. Even though I had completely mastered the moves of both the two-toed and the three-toed sloth, my days of rampaging through the jungle were pretty much forgotten—that is, until a few years ago.

I was back home visiting my father just after Christmas. By this time he had been an elder in that same childhood church for over thirty years, so it was not surprising when the phone call came to him that a longtime parishioner had passed away. He was always among the first to know. I remembered the woman quite well. Her name was Rosa, and she was the volunteer librarian for the church's fledgling library. There wasn't much to it when she started: some old, crusty commentaries, a few forgotten sermon compilations, and some loose assorted editions of *The Firm Foundation* and *The Gospel Advocate*. Most evenings you would find Rosa at the end of the long library table, putting Dewey decimal points on books that probably weren't worth reading, but we all remembered Rosa most of all because she made the best custard pies you ever tasted. At every parish potluck for forty years, people would race past the Jell-O salad and rice casserole and canned ham to get a wedge of one of Rosa's pies. They were legendary and worthy of every accolade. And she was the mother of my favorite Sunday school teacher, Mrs. Kindrick.

Although it had been years since I had seen her and I wasn't sure that a former star pupil who had become a heretic by defecting to the Episcopalians would even be welcome in her home, my father insisted that we stop by to pay our respects and offer our sympathies. Just like at the door to the three-year-olds' Sunday school class years before, I am so glad he didn't offer me a way out. "Let's go," he said.

Mrs. Kindrick welcomed us with the same warm openness she had as a Sunday school teacher. Within a few moments of our arrival, she reminded me of my cultlike status in her classroom, even now. "Billy, you sure could do that elephant walk when you were three. Why, you'd have that trunk just a-goin' all over the classroom." If Mrs. Kindrick had any idea about all the places that trunk had been over the last thirty-five-odd years, I am not sure whether she would have been proud or disappointed. But her affirmation was, and still is, a gift I will treasure for a very long time.

Then my earliest Sunday school teacher shared with us another gift and imparted one much later lesson. She told us the story of her grandson Joey's recent gift for his great-grandmother Rosa. It seems that by Christmas, Rosa was simply too weak and sick to get out of bed, and every Christmas for all of Joey's life, Rosa had baked for him his favorite custard pie. Since Rosa would not be doing any baking this year, Joey decided that he would do something unique for this special lady who had meant so much to him over the years. Twelve hours, a small fortune in ingredients, and a cluttered kitchen later, Joey finished making a custard pie for his great-grandmother using her secret recipe. With pride, he presented his creation to her on Christmas day, standing at her bedside and offering her this final gift. Rosa was too ravaged by disease to say anything, but a faint smile spread across her lips and her eyes filled with thankful tears.

These are the sweets that ultimately satisfy: the taste of gratitude, the flavor of giving. Like a homemade custard pie amidst a banquet of store-bought tidbits, such things stand apart and last for all eternity. I remember Tom Zakem, the man who never scrimped on the syrup and made the punch extra sweet each year at Vacation Bible School, enduring the wrath of the parents while winking at the enthusiastic children. I remember the cow-hoof soup the young woman prepared for me in a rural village in Honduras, so proud of her offering it tasted to me like filet mignon. I remember the swans who swim in the small pond near where my parents are buried, who whisper beauty in a place layered with reminders of morbidity. I remember my young, strong, determined father who knew when to let go and when to say no. I remember the realistic animal pictures on a classroom wall. And I remember when I didn't care if anyone was looking and I didn't need a pitcher of beer to make me move my feet to the beat of a favorite song. Such memories kind of make me want to dance.

Trunk out.

Feet apart.

Jungle beware.

CHAPTER 18

....

Dogma

Dogs need dogma. No complicated canine catechism is required, but critters, like all creatures, can benefit from a little training, admonition, and correction. Knowledge, especially in the spiritual and moral realm, is highly underrated.

Once Sam and I were walking on the trails around Town Lake in Austin when he committed some sort of unpardonable sin, some outrageous blasphemy capable of endangering his very soul, if not his rear. I don't remember exactly what it was because such is the nature of forgiveness—always to be taken with a healthy dose of Alzheimer's. Anyway, I reprimanded Sam immediately, yanking his chain, swatting his behind, and reinforcing my actions with a strong verbal cue ("You've violated Leviticus 23:12, again!"). A sweet, young, well-meaning but uninformed girl passed by at precisely that moment, paused, shook her finger in my face, and yelled, "You be nice to him. He's a sweetheart!" and continued on her way. While I instantly felt guilty of being possessed by the devil or at least exhibiting the behavior of a "meanie," the truth is I had done nothing wrong. And Sam had. The shocking news of the day was that even sweethearts sin!

In our time it may be countercultural to suggest that we should be as concerned about wrongs as rights. It may seem somewhat threatening to observe that just because certain actions come naturally to us, such ease of exhibition does not necessarily make them okay. Often, doing what comes naturally may feel quite unnatural for the recipient of nature's actions. While the cutest puppies on the planet may find it perfectly natural to eat another dog's excrement, to wallow in mud and then jump onto my bed, to bite all human feet that come within chomping distance of their mouths, to dig a breathtaking gorge in the middle of the neighbor's backyard, to hump the leg of the church secretary, and to rip all of the leather off my girlfriend's new couch, others may not be amused, entertained, or grateful. Nature is not always kind.

When Sam was a puppy, he wanted to taste everything: discarded candy wrappers, old gasoline canisters, all forms of sludge, and atomic waste products. If I allowed him, he would lick just about anything, including a clump of cacti. He was particularly fond of rocks. Piles of 'em. Whether igneous, sedimentary, stratified, or metamorphic, Sam found all kinds equally appetizing. If ever we were outside and I heard something crunching between his teeth, I could be reasonably certain it was not Bran Flakes, but chunks of earth. I would rush over to Sam, pry open his jaws, find the mineral culprit, shake his mouth until the dirty delicacy fell out, and then make a very big deal out of how terrible it was that he had tried to ingest such a solid. After a while, Sam got the point and quit eating rocks, which is probably in his best interest—and that of the earth's crust. Sticks, of course, are another story.

The first time Rachel brought Sam to the church office, he immediately found a comfortable spot under the large sofa and began chewing its legs off. The couch had been a gift from a church family, and it was frequently sat upon during all sorts of pastoral situations. The fact is, I needed that couch, and the couch needed its legs. By that time Sam and I had learned to communicate fairly effectively. He knew that if I raised a finger in the air and let out any sort of gasping sound, he was in serious trouble. If I followed these two signs by getting up out of my chair and heading in his direction, it was probably not to scratch his ears, tickle his tummy, or offer a treat. One finger raise and partial mouth gasp later, Sam looked very afraid and closed his mouth. He never chewed on the couch again, at least not while I was looking.

A few "thou shalt not"s never hurt anybody. Some things, such as murder, theft, injustice, rock eating, and couch-leg chewing are simply to be avoided. Nobody gains anything by doing them, and some may suffer greatly. Even if we "feel like it," we shouldn't engage in such potentially harmful behavior. Part of the process of spiritual maturity is the recognition of how our actions affect others and the boldness to help others sense such interconnectedness. What may be pleasing to my teeth may take the skin off someone else's back.

Sam can be stubborn and unruly, but generally he aims to please. Sam trusts me to steer him in the right direction. I can see in his eyes that he does want to do my will. He's no pushover. I just think he digs me. Whether you call this motivation love, relationship, intimate knowledge of the keeper of the treats, or just knowing who butters your bone, such a personal dynamic of trust is really the key to ethical behavior. Only when rooted in relationship does obedience mean anything.

Much of God's word to us seems ambiguous, culturally disguised, and conflicting. But the big stuff is all pretty clear to those onto the scent. Love God with all you've got. Love your neighbor (that's everyone else) as yourself. Act justly, embrace kindness, and walk humbly. Do not attempt to be the tail that wags the dog. In fact, even the Ten Commandments could be reduced to three simple statements: "Know that I am your master. Keep your paws (and your teeth) to yourself. Take regular naps." Perhaps not explicit instructions, but enough to keep us headed in the right direction. Knowing that God has been "off leash" longer than we can imagine and desires our well-being makes it much easier to trust and to obey. Desiring to please God is, in fact, quite pleasing to everyone involved.

One glorious spring Hill Country morning, I headed off toward Fredericksburg, a quiet little limestone town, with my new squeeze, a smart young Austin granola girl. This particular girl had it all: brains, cultural enlightenment, the ability to conjugate verbs in French, broad life experience, a kind heart, a master's degree, legs for days, long, brown hair, and a red sports car. She was feisty, philosophical, and not the least bit religious. She was no defender of the *status quo*, and she made secular humanism seem restrictive. In other words, she was perfect for me.

When I arrived at her ultra-hip, grunge/slacker/academic, yuppie-beware neighborhood bungalow to pick her up, she was sitting on her front porch step, drinking organic Nicaraguan coffee and strumming a Leonard Cohen tune on her guitar (badly, but she looked good doing it). She was wearing ragged blue-jean cutoff shorts (perfectly shredded), serious hiking boots (no doubt from Eastern Europe), and a tiny, tight V-neck All-American T-shirt (at last a hint of patriotism).

We had decided to spend the afternoon hiking around and eventually up to the top of Enchanted Rock, a mystical full moon–shaped, all-granite batholith (funny name for a big, protruding rock formation). First we stopped at a little German biergarten in Fredericksburg and enjoyed a Bavarian feast and several steins of grain-based German beverages. It was a perfect afternoon. As we began climbing up Enchanted Rock, I had trouble locating the trail marker.

Finally, I admitted my uncertainty, "I sure hope this is the right way up." My much younger, freethinking, less confined friend scoffed, "There is no right way up. It all leads to the same place." Since her particular style of boot was steel-toed, I decided not to argue, but I did cast dubious glances toward a couple of sheer drop-offs, an occasional cliff, some impossible terrain, and a few hiker-eating holes, all interspersed around the rock. Not wanting to suck the enchantment right out of our first formal date, I kept my mouth shut and kept climbing, all the way to the top.

Once we reached the summit, it was truly glorious. We were mostly alone. We had remembered to bring refreshing chilled beverages. The sunset was spectacular, the conversation stimulating. It was just cool enough she had to sit very close to me and request the windbreak of my arms. Now before I break into a chorus of "Some Enchanted Evening," let's just say that, somehow, we lost all track of time. For hours. Must have been the intense sharing of our personal testimonies. But probably not.

It gets very dark in the middle of nowhere. There were no lights anywhere, not even way down below in the direction of where we thought we parked our car. Even worse, instead of wearing my contact lenses, I had worn my prescription sunglasses, which were not so helpful for night vision. What such a decision meant for me was twofold: cool by day, blind by night.

"Don't worry," the free spirit reassured me. "I'll guide you down."

"You don't understand," I said. "I can't see anything at all—not even my own foot."

"It's okay," she told me. "Just hold onto me and go with the flow."

While I relished the thought of holding onto her the whole way down, I was absolutely mortified that my guide—the one upon whom my life now depended, the tracker who could, with one fatally misdirected step, send me plunging toward my death—was the very same girl who insisted that there was no right way up or down, that each direction was equally valid, that all paths were ultimately the same. At that moment, I desperately wished that I had learned to like cautious, fundamentalist girls. Sometimes staying on the straight and narrow is not such a bad idea.

While I understood her point that there was more than one way to the top and several different routes by which to get back down, I also recognized that some ways were far better than others. I was also pretty sure that more than one of the paths led nowhere—or somewhere much worse. Eventually she spotted a light and headed towards it. There was a sermon there somewhere, but I decided it was not the best moment to share my insights with her. It took us an eternity to reach level ground, and she still has an imprint of my hand on her stomach to remember me by. We stumbled some, backtracked on occasion, and changed direction at least once, but eventually we made it down. Even Ms. Carefree let out a sigh of relief and admitted a tinge of uncertainty there for a brief moment.

Later, as we continued to banter and spar over theological, philosophical, and political issues, her certitude seemed to loosen its grip. Maybe she began to realize that it was possible for there to be a wrong way up and a right way down or vice versa. Perhaps she gleaned that there were at least some preferable paths. Or maybe she just wanted me to shut up and kiss her.

I am always intrigued, but not for long, by those who are quick to give an opinion on some weighty matter without weighing it, without thinking it all the way through. There seems to be an abundance of those who do not yet know enough to know that they know nothing. Actually, I am not all that interested in what you think, *unless* you have read extensively, meditated continually, pondered passionately, and tested expansively. *Unless* you have struggled, argued, debated, wept, and changed your mind more than once. *Unless* you have consulted the traditions and contemplated the Scriptures. *Unless* you have processed the issue thoroughly with your maximum reasoning capacity and have drawn on all your varied life experience, as well as that of others. Then, I might care, because then, you might know something. But still not that much.

There is no particular code or absolute law or comprehensive doctrine that unlocks all mysteries and gives understanding of all matters. But I have found that some knowledge of the ancient sacred texts and the wisdom of the ages, some sense from the depths of my own soul, some counsel from my elders and those young enough to have hope, and some connection to a flesh-and-blood community of real, honest-to-God folks who shoot straight and tell the truth—*all* of these combine to keep me faithful, grounded, aware, and on track. And should I stray, I wouldn't mind at all if someone gave me a word of warning, a slight tug on my chain, or even a swat on my behind, if that is what it takes to get my attention. For it is helpful to know where I stand when I am oblivious, lost, headed the wrong way, in the dark, or in the middle of nowhere. In such situations, a little dogma can go a long way.

CHAPTER 19

....

Say Cheese

If Sam were ever to write a love song or compose a tender poem dedicated to the object of his affection (which he probably wouldn't because [a] though he is an excellent lyricist, the only note he can howl is a D, and monotone dog chants are hardly the rage, and [b] poetry strikes him as more of a feline pursuit), its subject would most likely be a yellowish-orange or sometimes cream-colored substance, well-aged, made from the milk of certain accommodating animals. The song would be some sort of blues riff, dedicated to the late, great blues musician Howlin' Airedale Muddy Paws "Damn Right I've Got a Tail" Hopkins. And it might go something like this:

Say Cheese

Woke up this mornin'
Had cheese on my mind
Took a little nap
Dreamed of cheese all the time.
Heard the fridge door open
I sprang to my feet
And ran to be ready
'Cause that cheese can't be beat.

Say cheese, pretty baby
Say cheese, pretty bovine babe
I'm udderly yours, sweet mama
Little milk cow, won't you marry me?

(Note: Grammy and Pulitzer Prize nominating committee members may forward Sam's nomination to me.)

Sam likes cheese. Not that Sam is averse to anything edible, with the exception of brussels sprouts and lamb. Other than these two exceptions in the entire known food chain, Sam is pretty enthusiastic about whatever is capable of being ingested. Here is how Sam would rate his top five foods, in reverse order:

5. Popsicles—tasty
4. Bacon—delicious
3. Any meat product, including rodents and rodent by-products—delectable
2. Bugs—divine, taste like chicken, except moister
1. Cheese—Oh my God! Did the earth just move?

I believe! Thank you, Jesus! There is a reason to live!

Well, bite my tail right off!

Who cares about sex or the playoffs or the scent of a yellow lab's ass? Sleep is highly overrated!

What? The moon is made of cheese?

5—4—3—2—1 . . .

When the refrigerator door opens, it matters not that I may be reaching for something quite dull like a Diet Dr. Pepper or a jar of olives. As long as there is a remote possibility that cheese may be involved, Sam will come running. Faster than Carl Lewis at a shoe sale, Sam will arrive from wherever he may be in record-breaking time and will sit without even being asked. In fact, he will plant his posterior on the floor so tightly you could not squeeze an easy-bake spatula under it. Should there be any sort of queso potential in this encounter with the refrigerated tabernacle, the repository of the blessed orange sacrament, Sam will maintain beauty-queen posture longer than it takes my system to fully digest and pass whatever snack I have scarfed down. He will sustain the pose until there is absolutely no hope that a hunk of tasty love will be carved from a cheese wedge and tossed his way. For Sam, Maslow's Hierarchy of Needs is about as essential as ambiguity is to a fundamentalist. What ultimately matters is Sam's Hierarchy of Cheese: American, Cheddar, Monterey Jack, Mozzarella, and Blue (by the way, "Blue Cheese Blues" would be the B-side of the "Say Cheese" single). According to Sam, there is truly a fine line between constipation and self-actualization.

Should I go as far as to actually remove the cheese from the refrigerator, though it remains tightly sealed in its plastic package, Sam's salivary glands could irrigate an entire desert. At the moment of cheese, the floor below Sam resembles Louisiana swampland; you'd need an airboat to make it across the kitchen to the microwave.

For Sam, cheese is the Great Motivator. Most of the time when I, in my most authoritarian alpha voice, tell Sam what to do ("Sit!" "Stay!" "Come!" "Make me a sandwich!"), he will perhaps glance in my direction before disregarding my orders and returning to his previously undisturbed activity. However, if I am holding a slab of cheese and I bark these same commands, he will instantly obey. (I rarely give the sandwich command anymore, because Sam finds it quite humorous to lick the bologna before placing it on the bread; and I won't even mention the ol' mustard trick he so enjoys.) The difference in Sam's behavior with and without cheese is the difference between snuggle bunnies and cacti, haloes and hand grenades. And whenever I do lecture him on proper motives or shove a thick copy of *Canines as Cultural Transformers in a Feline World* under his snout, he halfheartedly sniffs my shoe, rolls over, yawns loudly, and cuts some cheese. The bottom line for Sam fills his stomach more than feeds his soul.

I have discovered that the motives of many religious persons in our day are based primarily on a self-serving theology, a "what's in it for me?" brand of religious zeal. They "behave" mostly because they believe that in so doing they will, after this life, inherit a large chunk of cheddar in the sky, a sharp bye and bye, a sort of France-without-the-French version of paradise. Such persons act positively in order to feather their own afterlife nests and multiply their eternal portfolios. They milk the sacred dairy cows for all their own worth. They pose and posture for good works as the Almighty is busily snapping their photographs. "Say cheese," says the Lord, as they toss another ten bucks in the collection plate or slam on the brakes in their overpriced autos as they enter a clearly demarcated school zone. I am reminded of a bumper sticker I saw on the back of a Mercedes: "Don't be fooled by this car, my treasure is in heaven." Who's fooling whom?

Our "all about me" efforts to live just and righteous lives as long as the Great Refrigerator in the Sky is guaranteed to open for us reek of a moldy heart and reveal the theological substance of Cheese Whiz. Our souls become stunted, shrivel, and disappear from malnutrition when we try to subsist on such a diet of preprocessed spiritual food. Suffering through services we do not want to attend, performing ministries we have no desire to engage in, giving grudgingly, sacrificing halfheartedly, just so we can attain that giant bowl of cosmic queso in the big taqueria beyond, is a bizarre and perverse way to live. Being motivated by "God's blessing" is selfish, to say the least. Such cheesy admonitions may pad the bank accounts of the preachers who proclaim them, but abundance is clearly to be shared rather than sought. This much *all* the religious traditions make clear: there is no reward for acting out of ethical egoism. It is not, after all, about me. God does not reign mainly to meet my personal needs, and Christ does not live solely to be my "personal Savior." Now or in the life to come.

If the truth were told that righteousness is its own reward, would we quickly separate the curds from the whey? Would the goats quit giving milk, the sheep stop sharing wool, if the news leaked that there is no permanent pasture in paradise? What if there is no imperishable dairy farm just over the hilltop? What if, in the end, there is no cheese? Would houses of worship suddenly resemble a bachelor's refrigerator? If such realities would really change the way we think, live, and act, then we are guilty—as T. S. Eliot wrote—of committing the ultimate treason, doing the right thing for the wrong reason.

Years ago, Joseph Campbell observed of our culture that we no longer have heroes, only celebrities. I believe he was alluding to the difference between those who live by the searchlight (seeking the salvation of others) and those who live for the spotlight (seeking their own status among others). It is perversely fascinating to hear "celebrities for Christ" (a curious oxymoron) thank God on national television for paving their ways toward easy street. How many times have we heard the "winners" give God all the glory? What about the "losers" and the other true believers? Wouldn't it be refreshing to hear someone say on camera how difficult it has been to live according to God's standards? How they might have made the playoffs, or won the title, or been nominated for an award, if they hadn't been so distracted by the needs of others? How their lives had been downsized for the glory of God, their status knocked down a notch or two, and how often it sucks and they just wish God had left them to their formerly wild ways and indulgent devices? And how they long for the blessings they left behind when they decided to meet their maker on the maker's terms rather than their own? In some ways, it is the difference between eggs and bacon at the breakfast table. As a country preacher once pointed out, "The chicken may be involved, but the hog is totally committed." Now that's more information than most of us would like to say grace over.

There was a little boy at my church in Austin who once created quite a scene at the altar rail. Justin was around four years old and had not yet attended the First Communion class. Children are welcome to receive the Holy Sacrament anytime after baptism, but many parents choose to wait until their children have received sufficient instruction in its meaning and purpose. Therefore, many times when children come to the altar rail, they receive a blessing rather than the bread and wine, a literal pronouncement of God's love for them. The sign of the cross is made upon their foreheads, or a gentle hand is placed upon their noggins, or sometimes a simple bodily pat is given as the words of blessing are administered. Children are often instructed, as a sign to the priest that they wish to receive a blessing, to fold their arms across their chests rather than extend their hands openly to receive the eucharistic gift. Little Justin would have none of it. Ripping his hands right off of his upper arms after they had been yanked up there by his mother, he flailed toward a posture of reception, stood up on his tiptoes, thrust his hands toward me, and screamed, "I don't want a blessing! I want the Body of Christ!"

Perhaps never again will Justin utter words closer to the heart of God. If he is serious about such matters, if he is willing to forsake the blessing to receive the flesh-and-blood truth, he will be filled, satisfied, and sustained. He will receive a rich, flavorful life that will, indeed, last forever. For the aftertaste of such food never ends. It has no expiration date and does not require refrigeration. In fact—do not tell Sam—but I have heard that it tastes better than cheese.

CHAPTER 20

....

The One-Legged Bird and Other Normalities

Ilove to tease my friend Chuck Freeman, a Unitarian minister, about what you get when you cross a Unitarian with a Jehovah's Witness (someone who knocks on people's doors for no apparent reason), or about the Unitarian prayer that begins with: "To whom it may concern." That is not to say that Chuck is a man without firm convictions. On the contrary, Chuck feels strongly that Zima is a quality beverage, Larry Flynt is a prophet without honor in his own country, and that the North Carolina Tarheel is a deity worthy of its own religion. Nor is Chuck a man without passion. At the Bellagio Casino in Las Vegas, after losing a measly two hundred bucks at the blackjack table, Chuck brutalized an unoffending highback stool, sending it reeling into the gaming pit. For the record, Chuck still maintains, "I brushed up against the chair and it fell over." Chuck's nickname, "The Pimp" (among his friends, not his flock), has less to do with his sexual exploits than with his retro appearance (the mustache and gold chain do go well with the leisure suit). He also has a terrific sense of humor. "Well, I pulled another Jethro," Chuck will often admit the morning after some sort of disastrous evening excursion in the big city. For example, New Orleans has been a prime locale for such misadventures as reveal the inner hillbilly of this most sophisticated Unitarian.

One lovely fall afternoon in Austin, he and I were enjoying some Amy's Ice Cream outside on Sixth Street. Suddenly, Chuck, in his pimp voice, cackled "Hey, Billy, check that out!" Given Chuck's rare talent of spotting a hot girl a mile away, I figured that I would lay eyes on some exotic beauty.

Instead, my attention was directed to the sidewalk where a bird with only one leg was hopping forward. Not without effort, the bird methodically scoured the concrete landscape for a bit of sustenance. We watched intently as he finally snagged a share of a waffle cone still soggy with sweet cream, planted his one leg on the ground, stretched his wings, and soared into the sky. We ate our ice cream in silence and pondered the perseverance of the one-legged bird. It was a rare occasion in which Chuck did not offer some smart-ass wisecrack, but awe and appreciation were the order of the moment. Minutes passed in contemplation. Finally, Chuck, sympathetic to the plight of all creatures and always on the lookout for the spiritual significance of real-life events, offered, "I don't know what you're thinkin', but I'm thinkin' KFC!"

Several times I have participated in surveys in which the group question was posed: "If you could possess one supernatural power, what would it be?" Though I have consistently opted for the rare ability to understand why people drink lite beer, the overwhelming majority of participants typically wanted to be able to fly. I am not surprised. At the heart of spiritual yearning, holy questioning, and soulful longing is this innate desire to reach toward the heavens, to overcome the gravity of our respective situations, to scale the height of any obstacle blocking our view, and to soar above our mundane lives. Lack of parts does not preclude reaching a higher altitude. The good news is that even bird brains can learn how to fly. Yet we continue to hide in the hangar for fear of pulling a Jethro or being found out.

Our fear of heights is more often the fear of overcoming our inadequacies. Being tethered to the familiar rut in the ground in which we've made a comfortable home is much safer than learning to flap our underdeveloped wings and take off without a proper navigational system. Building nests on the ground, we need not worry about falling very far. Having our legs cut out from under us is a wonderful reason to crawl right back into the burrow of our discontent. Or we could hop along despite our disadvantages, keep looking until we find something that satisfies, plant our one good leg on any scrap of solid foundation, and take off. Birds of a feather may flock together. Birds without them can still improvise on their own.

My second-grade teacher, Mrs. Spinks, divided our classroom at the Garden Oaks Elementary School into three distinct reading groups: the Bluebirds, the Redbirds, and the Yellowbirds. I put them in this order because it is the order of their superiority. I, of course, was a Bluebird. In our minds, we were the fastest, smartest, most prolific readers in the room. Seeing Dick and Jane run was so yesterday's news for all of us Bluebirds. On the playground, Kent Adams, a fellow Bluebird, raised the previously unspoken question of the ranking of the three groups, so obvious to everyone with any sense of bird-reading skills. I was stunned to discover during a routine game of kickball that there was widespread disagreement among the students over the rankings of the various colored birds. Several of the Redbirds emphatically defended their group as being number one, while even a couple of lowly Yellowbirds, unbelievably oblivious to the company they kept, insisted that they were the top birds and could read circles around the Bluebirds.

Of course, such opinions were ludicrous, and so, upon our return to the classroom, several Bluebird hands shot up in the air and requested that Mrs. Spinks settle the score, revealing to all the birds the true significance of their colors. Being much wiser than the hatchlings in her class, Mrs. Spinks suggested that the real issue at stake here was not ornithological. Instead, each bird was beautiful in its own way, and could hatch, develop, and learn to fly (or read) at its own pace. She said that differences in rates of progression were not equivalent to distinctions in merit or aptitude, or something like that. A heavy blue cloud descended upon our egos and kept them momentarily grounded. Dammit, all we knew was that yellow was not a color to be taken seriously!

Spiritually speaking, most of us are reading the signs at about a second-grade level, so arguing over our belonging to the better group does not really call for the chirping of our praises. The point is that we're learning to read—or fly, or try, at our own personal pace. And whether I am the bird with one leg, the horse with no name, the dog with no tail, the cat with no attitude, or the dude with no date, I join a long line of seekers who seem to be missing something. That missing link has not stopped us or meant the end of the story. Failure to achieve in the field of aviation has less to do with ability and image than with resilience and resolution. So in the end, I suppose that the spiritual quest greatly resembles that one-legged bird; it might look pretty weird, but it can still manage to get off the ground.

Sam knows precisely what it means to be prejudged and to be taken less seriously than he should be. He can't help it that he is surrounded by fur that is naturally curly, possesses an almost human facial expression that is quirkily comical, and is often mistaken for a stuffed animal. He is the Rodney Dangerfield of dogs—the pet that gets no respect. He is quite familiar with the meaning of the phrase "laugh at first sight." One time Sam and I were minding our own business on a walk when a young slacker approached us with a prideful smirk and observed, "Sir, don't you think it's a bit inhumane to give a dog a full-body perm?" Little did the slacker suspect that underneath those silly curls was a serious survivor who bore battle scars. Sam could've simply thrown in the towel along with his ears. Instead, he has chosen the path less sniffed, to persevere despite what's missing. What's there is more important than what isn't. And that may not make him Einstein (or a Bluebird), but it does put him right up there with, say, the Rev. Freeman—mostly observant, certainly entertaining.

My ex-girlfriend Rachel, back when we were in that phase of our relationship when she would cradle my head in her lap and become mesmerized by my mere presence, once said to me, strangely, "Bill, if you ever lost an arm or a leg, I wouldn't mind."

"Well, I sure as hell would!" I retorted romantically.

Rachel laughed and attempted to clarify her position. "What I mean is, it wouldn't bother me."

"Well, it would damn sure bother me!" I clarified my own position. (Note to couples who may be reading: Although poor communication skills must be resolved, always seek to find humor in such exchanges. Second note to couples: Rachel and I lasted only two years, but that's more than a decade according to Sam.)

Anyway, in her own slightly distorted though endearing way, Rachel was trying to tell me that true love sees past the limitations, transcending appearance and ability. That even without legs, one could still get around. Even without wings, one could still take flight.

And if not, oh well, choices remain.

Original?

Or extra crispy?

PART THREE

· · · · · · · · · · · ·

New Dog, Old Tricks

CHAPTER 21

. . . .

Asses I Have Known

Back in the good ol' days of the King James Version of the Holy Bible, donkeys were referred to by their much more colorful name, "ass." This fact is important Bible trivia. You will want to share with your nonbelieving friends such inspirational information as this: the word "ass" is used in Holy Scripture a total of 137 times. "Ass" is mentioned in the Old Testament, a book more blatantly indelicate. than a Howard Stern interview, 129 times. The New Testament, a comparatively reserved collection of spiritual writings, features the a-word eight times. While that may not seem like many, it's mentioned seven more times than the word "upright." The even more provocative term "wild ass" is quoted an amazing eleven times in the Bible, all in the Old Testament. The word "asshole," however, while not to be found in translations of either sacred text, may be inferred numerous times from both the Hebrew and Greek versions.

This accounting brings me to my favorite Bible story, Balaam's Ass. Chronicled in the twenty-second chapter of the often overlooked but consistently titillating book of Numbers, this single story registers a record-breaking use of the word "ass" fourteen times, more than ten percent of all "asses" in the entire canon of Scripture. This bizarre tale of a faithful prophet and his talking sidekick never fails to entertain, if not enlighten.

In case you are unfamiliar with the story, it goes something like this. Once upon a time, Balak, Son of Zippor, and mighty king of Moab, started freakin' out because the Israelites, who had become bored while wandering in the wilderness and had just seriously kicked the Amorites' collective ass, had wandered toward Moab and camped right next to Balak's property line. Of course the Bible does not say that Balak "started freakin' out." The Hebrew literally states that Balak "got his panties in a wad." So Balak gathered up the elders of Midron (i.e., his poker buddies), and, fearing that his people were going to get a good licking by the Israelites, said, "This horde will now lick up all that is around us, as an ox licks up the grass of the field." The ol' ox-licking-grass metaphor was always one to put fear in the hearts of his hearers. Balak sends messengers all the way to Pethor on the Euphrates River, in the land of Aman to summon the relatively famous prophet/diviner/highly intuitive guy Balaam, sort of an Amazing Kreskin with a collar. Balak offers Balaam a hefty consulting fee for merely placing a little curse on the Israelites, but Balaam is the real deal and refuses to engage in false prophecies even for the sake of dramatically higher profit margins. Balak's buddies return to tell him, "Balaam won't budge!"

Once more, Balak sends a group to convince Balaam to do the dirty deed. This time, the delegation includes the five finalists from the Miss Moab pageant. Balaam, taking his calling seriously, consults with the Big Guy and concludes that God desires blessing for the fledgling people of Israel. So he announces, "Though Balak offered me all the money in Moab and Midian, even if he should throw in a gold-covered chariot with plush camel hair interior, I calls 'em likes I sees 'em. Survey says: blessing not curse!"

That night, God appears to Balaam in a dream and tells him to go with the celebrity posse to Moab, provided that he does only what God tells him to do. The next morning, Balaam saddles up his ass and rides just behind the official caravan, positioning himself coincidentally, but strategically, within eyesight of Miss Moab's backside. Then the story gets as confusing as, say, doing God's will. The very next verse says, "God's anger was kindled because he was going, and the angel of the Lord took his stand in the road as his adversary." Excuse me, but didn't God command Balaam to go? And now God is angry because Balaam did what he was told to do!

Balaam does not see the avenging angel with a drawn sword in his hand. (Note to collectors who find angel kitsch irresistible:

real angels carry big swords and are not afraid to use them!) However, Balaam's ass, blessed with angel-vision, sees the winged, armed obstacle and heads for the nearest field. Balaam wallops the ass with a two-by-four to get it back on track. Next, the angel appears in a narrow upcoming path between some vineyards where there is a wall on either side. The ass, knowing the blade is more painful than the board, scrapes against one of the walls, slamming Balaam's foot into the same barrier. Again, Balaam beats his former friend with the paddle. Then the angel moves up to an opening about as wide as a donkey's tail. When the ass sees the unavoidable collision ahead, it comes to a halt and decides to lie down right then and there with Balaam still on its back. For the third time, Balaam spanks his ass.

The donkey has had enough. He finally says to Balaam (the Scripture says that the Lord opened the mouth of the ass), "What have I done to you that you would hit me thrice?" Actually the donkey said "three times," but frankly a donkey saying "thrice" makes for good reading. Balaam tells the donkey that it has made a fool out of him and that if he had a sword in his possession, he would kill the donkey on the spot. The ass replies, reminding him of their kinship, "Am I not your ass, on which you have ridden your entire life? And have I previously treated you this way?" Balaam says, far less eloquently than the ass, "Uh, no."

Then Balaam's eyes are opened, and he sees the source of the donkey's dilemma. The angel points out the error of his ways: "That donkey just saved your ass. If your four-legged friend hadn't changed directions, I would have taken a sword to your thick head and let the ass pass."

Balaam acknowledges his mistake, saying, "Me bad. Ass good. Say the word and I'll go home." The angel reiterates what God had already told Balaam in the dream: go on ahead, but speak only what God tells you to speak. This makes about as much sense as a talking ass.

The rest of the story is not nearly as interesting. Balaam goes to Moab, and given three different opportunities by the king to pronounce a curse, he blesses Israel every time. He returns home. The Scriptures do not say which prophet (human or animal) got a lift back. My guess is Balaam's shoulders were real tired by the time he and the Reverend Doctor Donkey returned to Pethor.

Surely, there is a profound theological point in this wonderfully strange story, but I'm not entirely certain what it is. I suppose we could observe a few almost asinine truths: (1) If it's unclear and contradictory, it's probably the Word of the Lord. (2) God has a right to change God's mind without telling us about it. (3) Don't get cuddly with an angel unless you're prepared to lose a limb. (4) Endurance, a root of the Hebrew word for "ass," will eventually take us home. (5) Blessings can't be bought. However, based on this story, there is only one thing we can say with absolute certainty while standing on solid theological ground. The Almighty God is most assuredly able to speak through the mouth of an ass.

That's good news for me. Otherwise I'd probably be out of a job.

I have known asses. For much of my life, I have encountered them. On the road to Moab. On the way to Piggly Wiggly. From the boardroom to the bedroom. Within the city and far out in the country. From the big and hairy to the taut and tiny, I have known asses. Some were simply mules in ass's clothing. Others were real asses. Some lived on farms. Others lived right next door. A few have been asked to kiss my own. And all are worthy of the name.

The first time I heard my mother, a proper southern woman, refer to someone by this name, it was an epiphany that "ass" could be used as a term of endearment. Although on rare occasions she would call an inconsiderate person or a misbehaving son a "horse's ass," in general her use of the word was quite positive.

I was nine years old when my brother Tom had returned home from his freshman year in college with his roommate in tow. Jack Arvin was a tall, lanky Texan from Fort Worth via Baytown. He had massive sideburns, which my friends and I thought were very cool. Beyond the normal scale of mutton-chops, he had longer-than-face Brontosaurus chops, which were dated but hip. Jack also possessed the slowest, thickest, deepest Texas drawl I had ever heard. When Jack traveled with Tom to Mexico, it was reported that crowds gathered whenever Jack opened his mouth. I had never known anyone in real life to speak in slow motion. Although grade-school film projectors made Clifton Fadiman sound ready to bellow up a giant syntax monster from the deep recesses of his internal encyclopedia at the speed of a slug, such sounds were unnatural and technologically garbled. Jack's words seeped like honey from a hive: thick, syrupy, and sweet. The most interesting exchange on the block, for which my friends would all come over and listen intently, was between Jack's deep, friendly, mellowing drawl and my mother's excitable, high-pitched East Texas swamp rattle.

Recognizing that Jack's nickname was Jack Ass, shortened by his college buddies to the succinct, but expressive "Ass," my mother would graciously welcome Jack into our home with a rapid-fire series of greetings/questions/admonitions that sounded something like, "Well, Ass, howeryoudoingitisgoodtoseeyouhowerthosegradesareyoutakinggoodcareofmysonhoneycomeinhere-Tom'shomefromcollegeandhe—brought—Ass—with—him."

Ass would reply, taking ten minutes to connect these words, "HowwdeeeeeMizzzMiiiillerrrr."

Their conversations entertained us for hours. Like an okra-cooking contest, fried vs. gumbo, my mother would toss her diced and battered fragments into the bubbling skillet, searing dozens of words at a time, cracklin', dancin', and done before you could shake salt into the cornmeal, while Jack would counter with a sluggish, simmering gumbo on the far backburner, stirring in one giant stalk of the slimy southern vegetable at a time. By the time Jack brought a sentence to a slow boil, my mother would've fried up a truckload of bushel baskets filled with random paragraphs, ramblings, fragments, and voluminous observations on just about everything, all the while addressing Jack matter of factly in a church-lady sort of way, "Well now, Ass, blah, blah, blah." I am still not sure which was more remarkable, the contrast in communication styles or hearing my mother repeatedly refer to a fine, young Christian man as "Ass." Jack tolerated such potential abuse with the poise of a trusty steed or at least an honest mule. He was polite throughout all of these verbal ordeals, not in a contrived Eddie Haskell way, but with the utmost sincerity, humility, and truth. He behaved as unlike an ass as anyone I have ever known.

I had not seen Jack in at least twenty-five years, and my brother had finally lost track of him as well. There were rumors of an M.B.A., a law degree, a biker lifestyle, and even a marriage (all unsubstantiated). One day, I was doing bicep curls at my health club in Austin when I spotted an unusual-looking dude giving the free weights a major workout. This guy stood out from the typical computer geeks, granola heads, and yoga freaks who frequented this establishment in the silicon hills. His upper arms, the size of canned hams, intimidated me into returning my tiny dumbbell to the toddler weight section. His head was shaved except for one braided plug that poked out of the back of his head and dangled about a foot below his twenty-seven-inch neck. His facial hair, for which there must be some sort of martial arts–style name, screamed, "Go ahead and make fun of me and I'll calmly break your head as I continue to lift weights and read this very large book which I am balancing between my legs." He was massive, chiseled, and he sweated testosterone. His body shape was to the average male physique what a beef rib is to a Slim Jim—substantive. He wore a black shirt with the sleeves ripped out. On the back it said in bold print, "I Beat Bulimia!" Who was I to argue?

He spoke.

Twenty-five years later, it was still the deepest, slowest, thickest Texas drawl I had ever heard. Although he looked nothing like that lanky, lamb-chopped college freshman, I'd have recognized that voice anywhere. I approached him waving a white T-shirt in case he misinterpreted my advance and tried to crush me. I revealed my identity, and he shook my hand, almost dislocating several of my fingers, as he shook his head in disbelief. "How the hell did you recognize me?"

"The voice, Jack," I told him.

He nodded, smiled, and chuckled in slow motion. He was still just as gracious as I remembered him, as he asked about my folks and my brother's family. We exchanged phone numbers and several weeks later Jack met my brother, his wife, children, and me at a local restaurant. Still a man of few words, he wouldn't reveal too much, but he had done quite well with some investments and told us about his present lifestyle. "I read books, sculpt, and lift weights—that's pretty much it." Some guys are just born to be cool. He insisted on picking up the tab, cleanly jerking a weightlifter's wad of C-notes from his front pocket. Alas, my mother would have been proud of Ass.

Appearances aside, nomenclature be damned, there are some people in the world who are the anti-asses: kind, thoughtful, gracious. They care about the things that matter and don't care about the things that don't or about your opinions regarding such things. They often speak with accents, possess unique nicknames, and have diverse interests. They live their own lives, blame no one for their plight, treat everybody with dignity and respect, and never fail to see the humor in a situation. They speak slowly and listen intently. They make a mean gumbo. And they will kick your ass only if you absolutely deserve it, which you probably do.

Years ago, after several days of hiking in the Swiss Alps, my buddy Michael Soper and I boarded a Swiss train, tossed our grimy backpacks into the overhead luggage compartment, and sprawled out in our near-empty passenger car. The Swiss do several things incredibly well: scenery, chocolate, and cheese, to name three. They also know how to run a rail line: clean, well-appointed, and on time just like Swiss clockwork. Being the unconscientious American that I sometimes am, I propped my muddy hiking boots up on the seat in front of me, getting comfortable for the long trip, while smearing mountain muck on a seat cushion that might eventually belong to another weary traveler. The porter observed my breach of rail passenger etiquette and politely asked me to remove my feet from the adjacent seat. I obliged. Time passed. I didn't notice that my boot-laden feet had, of their own accord, propped themselves back up on the seat cushion that did not belong to me. The porter came by again and, aghast at my insensitivity and disregard for decency, threw his hands up in the air, made a slight gasping noise in the back of his throat, and walked briskly out of the compartment.

Being from Texas, I knew exactly where he had gone. He had gone to get either (1) a very large law officer who would verbally humiliate, physically pummel, and forcefully arrest me, or (2) a gun with which to shoot me. I braced for the inevitable punishment about to be inflicted upon me. Within moments he returned with something in his hands. Assuming that it was some sort of a weapon, I winced. It was a large paper towel. He boldly approached the seat cushion across from me, spread out the towel, patted it down flat, and gently maneuvered my boots onto the paper protector. He wiped his hands together, smiled at me, and departed.

Add civility to the Swiss list. That day I learned something about manners and about basic human decency. They do exist.

For every inconsiderate ass in the world like me, there is at least one really nice guy out there. Somewhere. Perhaps in Switzerland.

There is one day each year on which we allow our liturgical leader to have hooves. On perhaps the most schizophrenic Sunday on the Christian calendar, Palm Sunday, also known as Passion Sunday, worshipers follow a donkey in procession. This particular feast day abruptly shifts from celebratory joy to painful introspection, from Jesus' triumphant entry into Jerusalem to the utter isolation of Calvary's crucifixion. One moment we who worship are loyal fans at a sporting event; the next we're a group of sociopaths demanding death. The adoring crowd that waved palm branches and shouted, "Blessed is the one who comes in the name of the Lord!" is suddenly transformed into an angry mob screaming, "Crucify him! Crucify him!" The dramatic turn of the event actually nails us, for it is just like you and me to embrace such extremes.

Questioning our own sanity we ask ourselves: Should I wave a palm frond or pound a nail? Am I a cheerleader or a killer? An angel or an ass? Before we can figure out our true identities, whether we are ready or not, here comes Jesus, the supposed Savior of the world riding into town on the back of an ass. Not just any ass, but an insignificant one. Jesus chooses neither the Grand Prize Winner from the 4-H Club Donkey Committee nor the Blue Ribbon Pick of the County Fair. This little fella wouldn't even make the circus sideshow. He is talentless, slow, and remarkably unremarkable. He does not talk. His legs wobble under the weight of the grown man who looks ridiculous riding him. He should be ashamed, and so should we.

One Palm Sunday at St. James in Austin, my friend Suzanne McCord brought two of her prized miniature Sicilian donkeys named Dolly Parton and Sophia Loren to lead our procession. Gentle and cooperative, Dolly and Sophia even displayed dark fur markings on their backs that formed the shape of a cross. Right up until the service began, the children gathered for donkey rides. Outside it was just like an old-fashioned carnival, while indoors, the turn of events was strangely reminiscent of the attached freakshow.

When the procession finally arrived at the front doors of the church, Dolly and Sophia did not enter, but moved to a grassy area to graze, while the rest of us walked right on in to participate in the dirtiest deed of all. During the reading of the Passion Gospel, the congregation assumes the role of the crowd that clamors for the crucifixion of our Lord. Though we may initially protest our presence and wonder why we're here, our words and actions begin to become strangely familiar. Beyond mere role-playing, we seem to know this moment and these people, and ourselves all too well. We are on the inside, looking out at our four-legged friends. It is blessed irony that donkeys are forbidden, and asses are allowed.

CHAPTER 22

············

I Know Jack

Sam was not to be outdone the summer I visited Bulgaria. He went to Oklahoma. He stayed there for only a few hours and slept in the back seat of the car for the majority of the journey. However, he came back with a souvenir that would forever change his life—a rowdy little Airedale pup named Jack—the little brother he had not known he had missed all these years.

When Sam was six years old I accepted the position of rector of Trinity Church and moved back to Houston from Austin. So, Sam began to commute. Once a month, Rachel and I would meet at either the gas station/burger joint outside of Columbus on Highway 71 or the gas station/ice cream stand outside Brenham on Highway 290. As compensation for her meeting me halfway, I would buy Rachel a brisket sandwich or some Blue Bell ice cream. It was a good deal for all of us. I saved three hours of driving; Rachel got free food; Sam got to lick the bowl.

During those weeks when Sam was visiting me in Houston, Rachel discovered that she was not called to the solitary life. She was lonely. She missed the companionship of our boy. She also theorized that Sam, alone in the tiny studio apartment during her workweek, must be experiencing some of the same feelings of isolation and emptiness. What Sam needed was a brother, a pup who could keep him company while she was at work during the day and who could be a surrogate Sam to her when Number One Son was visiting me. So, off they went one afternoon, all the way to Oklahoma.

Rachel had been told by the breeder beforehand that only the runt of the litter was available, but the hairiest of the lot, a solid little guy they named Tank, quickly endeared himself. This particular pup was, in the words of the breeder, "too white to be a show dog." While Rachel and I agree that too much white is rarely a positive phenomenon, this little fella's bleachy tufts on chin and belly and his Comiskey Park–caliber white sox on the bottoms of all four feet made him as cute as can be.

"What about this one?" Rachel asked as the outgoing tyke ran over and introduced himself, demonstrating his athletic prowess by bucking like a bronco and resting his chin on her leg.

"Well, someone already claimed him," the breeder said, "but I told 'em if they didn't leave a deposit, I couldn't guarantee anything."

Rachel laid out a wad of cold, hard cash right on the spot. Soon, white boy was nuzzled up to his big brother in the back seat of the Jeep ready for the ride back to Texas.

By that time, Rachel's love life had taken a turn for the, well, more interesting. She was seeing a former All-Pro NFL linebacker who had just won the lottery. No, I am not making this up. Reality is much more interesting than fiction. Technically, this man is Jack's financial father as he paid for more than 50 percent of his purchase. However, I'd also like to thank the risk-takers of Texas for the lottery winnings that helped secure Sam's brother. Before long this football star relinquished all parental rights and responsibilities. Soon after that, Rachel began dating a former All-Pro defensive end who would later pursue a career in boxing. Truth is stranger than make-believe. Too bad the boys didn't get their trust funds set up while they had their chance.

Rachel named Number Two Son Andrew Jackson, deferring to her Tennessee roots and the fact that she is related to the former two-time president and Southern war hero, even named after his wife. Supposedly, the namesakes of the two dogs, Andrew Jackson and Sam Houston, were friends in real life. Therefore, it was fit-

ting that Sam and "Jack," as Rachel dubbed him, bonded immediately. Jack had a brother; Sam had a friend. And with two
Airedales in the house, Rachel had more male companionship
than the entire Doomsday defense of the Dallas Cowboys.

Even an introvert like me understands the need for relationship. As in life, so it goes with religion. There are those who claim
that their spirituality is a private matter of no interest to anyone
but themselves that they can work out on their own time, by their
own rules, on their own turf. They miss out on such significant
components as partnership, companionship, and community.
Some things are just better when shared. This includes faith.
Thomas Merton said that we do not find the meaning of life by
ourselves alone—we find it with another. We are made for mutuality; loving another is our ultimate destiny as human beings.
While our need for human connection may find its fulfillment in
an individual or an entire community, what is important is that
our spiritual journey is shared with those beyond ourselves.

Just as Sam and Jack discovered that life is more fun by hanging out with a bud, and Rachel recognized that love is more interesting by dating half the roster of the '82 Pro Bowl, so I am coming
around to the realization that I need someone else too. It is not
that I am somehow incomplete, or that I naively believe that there
is only one human being out there with whom I could enjoy a fulfilling relationship. It's just that sometimes I need someone to
scratch that itchy spot in the center of my back, and to throw up
their arms and say to me, "You're *not* wearing/eating/drinking/
buying/displaying/watching/reading/writing/preaching *that*, are
you?!" I tend to live a little rough around the edges. Applicants
need to know how to operate a sander and not be afraid to use it.

Sam and Jack bonded big-time. Jack had a large, furry, four-
legged mattress on which to rest his head, and a wiser soul to look
up to for guidance, knowledge, and the occasional reprimand.
Sam had a playmate, someone to wrestle, chase, and play tug-of-
war with when the humans were off doing that pointless thing
called work. Rachel and I had no idea just how close Sam and Jack
had gotten until Sam came for his first visit since Jack's arrival.

Everything started out just fine. Sam did not hesitate to jump
into the truck because he was happy to see me, but his appetite
seemed a bit depressed as he ate with far less enthusiasm. When we

got back to the house he was much more lethargic and lazy than was his custom. He immediately went to sleep and would not budge for hours. I knew he couldn't have been homesick for his mother. Perhaps he had the stomach flu or was upset that I had washed the sheets since his last sleepover. In truth, he missed his little brother. Sam recognized that life is much more lively when shared with a partner in crime.

Back in Austin, Little Brother had it even worse. On Jack's first day without Sam, the neighbors complained that he had howled without ceasing from the time when Rachel left for work until she came home. He had cried with all the force his little lungs could muster for ten straight hours, pausing only to inhale. Around Sam, Rachel reported Jack had been cocky, brave, and curious. After that day alone she found him looking like a fearful little puddle of vulnerability, head buried in a pillow, as limp and lifeless as a damp dishrag. All that sweat and tears combined to make this little Okie look as though he just paddled the length of the Red River.

Rachel called me and explained her predicament. A shock collar was out of the question. Losing her lease was not an option. She couldn't afford to miss work or to alienate the neighborhood. Could Jack please come and stay with Sam and me? Of course, this was not at all our agreement, but she would pay all of Jack's expenses including mileage and incidentals, send his toothbrush, puppy chow, and even come all the way down to get him should he turn out to be a bother. It was my lucky day—two dogs for the price of three!

My sense of patriarchal duty overtook me, and I agreed to adopt Jack and raise him properly. It was obvious from the beginning that Jack needed a human male in his life, a firm voice and strong hand to guide him in the ways of the Lord. Rachel had never taken him to church or made him memorize the books of the Bible. I once sang "Jesus Loves the Little Puppies" to him, but he didn't know the words. I had a mission.

Jack and I immediately connected, and I was highly amused from day one by Jack's antics. He is, as Rachel calls him, "the scholar/athlete of the family." He swam like Tarzan during our first dip in Barton Creek. He scales heights that no other dog can approach. He leaps over tall furniture in a single bound. Most hilarious of all is watching Jack utilize the "Sampoline." While Sam is standing there on all fours, unsuspecting and unaware, Jack gets a running start, leaps up and plants himself on Sam's back, using it as a springboard to jump over the couch or anything else in his way. Sam's a good sport about it, but Jack is definitely the superior athlete. Sam is an athletic supporter to Jack's Olympic champion.

Also amusing are the WWF-caliber wrestling matches that take place in my living room. Sam may be bigger, but Jack is much faster. Each animal uses a variety of well-staged wrestling maneuvers, especially whenever the highly coveted Rib Belt is at stake. Sam employs such moves as the Bulldozer, the Belly Flop, and the Neck Chomp. Jack's quickness allows him to get away with the Tail Bite, the Leg Grab, and my personal favorite, the Top Dog Leap— a lightning-bolt strike (highly illegal) that looks much like a traditional Sampoline mount. However, once on board, Jack embeds his claws in Sam's back and rides him around the room like a cowboy conquering a bull at the O.K. Corral.

Sometimes I am tempted to take the role of the overprotective father during these no-holds-barred living room brawls, worrying that somebody's going to get hurt. Then I remember that it is all for show. Although it may look like an all-out war, a duel to the death, on about every other move, either Sam or Jack will look around to make sure that they still have an audience. No audience, no performance. Should something distract me momentarily, they turn it up a notch until they have my undivided attention. While I believe that they sometimes wrestle purely for the sport of it, they are generally poised for prime time, more concerned about looking good doing it than holding their opponent down for the full count. If they realize that I have not been watching for a prolonged period of time, they'll simply stop until I have tuned back in. Entertainment value takes precedence over physical prowess.

At such moments, Sam and Jack remind me of those religious sorts who consider it a real courageous stand, a brave battle against the forces of wickedness, to wrassle up some public display of piety. Fearlessly embracing such causes as the overt display of religious symbolism, the visible posting of Christian commandments, formal prayer in educational or civic settings, and turning science textbooks into devotional material, they seem to think they're engaged in a real Olympic event, heeding God's call to kick butt for Jesus. The problem is that Jesus never advocated such showy posturing. In fact, Jesus was pretty much consistently opposed to public displays of personal religious practices. When you pray, he said, don't try to get everyone's attention. Just the opposite: go into your own private closet and shut the damn door, and keep your voice down lest someone hear you. There is no rule anywhere to stop you or anyone else from praying in the way Jesus recommends. When you fast, Jesus said, or make any sort of sacrifice for religious reasons, don't put your good deed on parade or call attention to what you are doing. Not at all. Even if you've starved yourself for a week to feed your soul or groveled in dirt to remind yourself of your own inadequacies, dress up, bathe, and comb your hair. Don't go around looking emaciated. Wear something flattering. Otherwise, you already have your reward, and it's about as big a deal as a chrome-plated plastic trophy.

Unlike some religious zealots, at least Sam and Jack are entertaining in the wrestling ring and are very much aware that it's all for show. Nobody gets hurt, and everybody has a little fun in the process. Though pretend, it's a pretty good workout. And in the end, the Rib Belt has value beyond its symbolism. Not only can it be worn around the waist, it can be eaten as well!

Although the flashy scheme may get all the attention, we learn a lot more about the weightier matters of religion when we're out of the public eye, behind the contrived scenes, relating to one another simply for the sake of relationship. In these interactions, we discover the value of timeless truths such as forgiveness and faithfulness. These values are not merely for show. They are real, and they are worth fighting for. The reward for being true to our partners in crime is the knowledge that we have true partners, regardless of the crime. Jack has taught me much about such things.

When Jack's around, it's not all spotlights and charm. He can test your limits and wear out his welcome. There have been numerous occasions when he has been one dog-hair shy of solitary confinement. Once, he nearly got killed darting in front of a car while chasing beagles across the street. Another time at the bay house while deeply contemplating a sermon I was roused by a hysterical neighbor who barged in shouting, "You got a dog overboard, man!" Jack had decided to take his chances à la *Escape from Alcatraz*, dove into the canal, and swam toward a nearby neighbor dog. When the Good Samaritan next door tried to nab him, Jack swam up a boat ramp and darted down the street. For several tense moments I worried that Jack had been swept out to sea or gotten stuck in a boat slip or devoured by a shark. Finally, I found him four houses down, peering at me from behind a palm tree, smelling of sea water and dead fish.

Jack saved his worst behavior for the church and rectory, however. He clawed the corners off a Tibetan rug, peed in the sacristy, nearly knocked over a little old lady at the parish potluck, and in a rare moment of pure, profane evil, pooped in the church! When a parishioner yelled at me for "allowing Jack to desecrate a sacred space," I reminded him that the space is desecrated every time he walks in. It's like when people refuse to go to church because the place is "filled with hypocrites!" I simply tell them, "There's always room for one more." What most people try to unload on religion or on the church makes Jack's offering look like a charitable endowment. May the one without sin pick up the poo.

Jack is like a troubled teen, excitable but loving—bad behavior, good heart. He craves attention and will crawl into your lap or give you a hug at any opportunity. If Jack is getting attention and Sam starts to stir on the other side of the room, Jack will spread his entire body across you, smothering all of you with affection and disallowing any portion of you to be exposed and available to any other dog. Jack insists on your undivided attention and goes nuts at the mere possibility that you might bestow it on someone else. I wonder if that's how God views religious folks who claim to hold exclusive rights to his touch and blessing. I suspect that God's lap is bigger than every attempt to fill it.

Once, after a particularly troublesome visit, when Jack had brought enough chaos into my life to last an entire liturgical season, Rachel listened to my litany of complaints. Jack had sinned, willfully and repeatedly. She offered to come to Houston and pick him up.

"No," I told her, "I think Jack and I still have some things to learn from each other."

"Well, Bill, you should have a lot in common with Jack," Rachel pointed out. "You're both bad boys."

Ouch—the sting of truth. I remembered one time I was compared to my older brother Tom, who is pretty much a better human being than I am in every way, even more so when we were kids. After I had made a big mess of something and gotten sassy with both my attitude and articulations, my grandmother turned to my mother and, within earshot of me, said, "Well, you had your angel when you had Tom!" I suppose she had her jackass when she had me. I once related this incident to my congregation, and they sighed audibly in unison. Pity the priest, and be amused by the blessed irony of God's call.

Jack has been a part of my life for several years now. Sam is still the proverbial man in my mind, but I have gotten to know and love Jack too. My fearless, earless Airedale and my little jackass. Jack's basic personality has not changed, but his attempts to please me have certainly intensified, and I suppose such efforts are enough. Like the New Orleans cab driver who related how he told his wife, "I won't gamble no more. And I won't gamble no less," change does not come easily for any of us creatures of habit. The wrestling matches continue, and so does an odd and potentially disgusting habit Sam and Jack have of cleaning each other's ears—with their tongues! Is this an image of pure, unconditional love? The sacrifice to which one is willing to go to assist those who are significant companions? Or is there some sort of perverted thrill transpiring in such moments? I am not sure. But I do know that love will go to great lengths—ear cleaning, poo picking, Sampoline serving.

Sam is more solitary than Jack, withdrawing to an isolated place at times in the day and night. Jack prefers to be where the action is, or at least where the action might be. He will let me know, subtly but clearly, when he wants to go outside to romp around, and he is unashamed to brazenly solicit attention. Sometimes Jack and I engage in what I like to call "Lap Prayer." It is similar to a lap dance (only cheaper and much more satisfying in the long term). Such a personal connection is not for show. True intimacy, religious or physical, is not really for public consumption. In these treasured moments, Jack will simply crawl up into my lap, spread out, and look deeply into my eyes while I scratch his butt. He will sometimes stretch, sigh, yawn, and lick me. It's sort of a mystical combination of meditation, gratitude, prayerfulness, and intimacy.

Few words are actually spoken. I may on occasion say, "I know you. I love you, man."

He rarely responds, except to say, "Bill, you're not getting my Rib Belt."

And that's okay. I already have my reward.

CHAPTER 23

••••••••••

All About Yaks

The Casino Royale at the Hotel Yak and Yeti in Kathmandu, Nepal, is what happens when John Waters meets *National Geographic*. Although my friend Jimmy Grace and I were anticipating the beginning of a challenging ten-day Tibetan trek, Jimmy the Blackjack Kid, and I, Big Money Miller, nevertheless decided to grace the casino with our presence for one final frivolous evening before the far more serious spiritual journey began. The night started appropriately with a decadent meal of delicious grilled meats and butter-flavored daal. Lucky for us our favorite Indian restaurant, Bukhara, happened to have a branch at the Crowne Plaza Hotel where we were staying. It was a fine choice for lodging and dining, but after a couple of Kingfisher beers we were ready to take our partying to the next level. The Hotel Yak and Yeti beckoned, promising to be as fascinating as its name.

After exchanging some dollars for Nepali rupees and discovering that the dealer advantage also applies to the money changer, we settled in at the blackjack table, determined to have a little fun without completely depleting our travel fund. The only other English-speaking gambler in the place, a gregarious young Singapore Airlines pilot, sat down beside us and exponentially increased the rowdiness factor of our threesome, so much so that the pit boss parked it nearby for the duration of the evening.

The Casino Royale was everything one could hope a casino in Kathmandu, Nepal, at the Hotel Yak and Yeti might be: freakishly bizarre. The cover band offered a rendition of "Hotel

California" so scary they should have called themselves the Yetis. Like this oddity of nature we sometimes refer to as "Bigfoot" or "the Abominable Snowman," their music-making was both frightening and frozen. I once heard a Soviet military rock band, in full uniform, perform precise, robotic versions of Eagles hits years before Gorbachev's *Perestroika* and the *glasnost* reforms loosened things up a bit over there. I'd have to say that the Yetis had even less soul, not to mention rhythm.

Other than the pit bosses and money changers, all of the employees were very attractive young women, divided into three groups based on physical beauty. The blackjack dealers were quite cute, the waitresses were very lovely, and the "helpers" were complete knockouts. The "helpers" were there for the sole purpose of creating a pleasant gaming atmosphere, thereby encouraging you to squander more resources on various games of chance. Should you have any questions regarding rules or wagering, the helper would make herself available to flirt over your shoulder, to explain any unclear aspects of the different games, and to whisper tantalizing casino strategies into your ear such as "I think you bet big this time, you American stud." So what if we just happened to increase our bets every time a helper came by? Much to the pit boss's dismay, we were winning.

In American casinos it is customary to tip your waitress. Since the drinks are free (actually if you count your losses against beverages consumed, it works out to about three hundred dollars per beer) and the waitress is nice enough to bring you your alcoholic beverage of choice, it is common to tip the waitress a dollar chip or so every time she comes by. Such tipping is not customary in Kathmandu. As all three of us were tipping our lovely waitress about a buck a beer, she was practically in Shangri-La every time she came near our table. We eventually did the math and figured out that if we'd spent a week there, our waitress could've retired. "Tank you. Tank you," she said breathlessly, arranging our beverages before us so as not to interfere with our towering piles of rupees. Finally, on her third visit, she smiled at us seductively and asked the question every man wants to hear at least once in his life. Looking at all three of us, she asked, "You wan sax?"

I choked on my beer. Jimmy stopped breathing. The pilot demanded clarification, "What did you say?"

Again she said to us gratefully but matter of factly, "You wan sax?" Although her English pronunciation was not particularly precise, there being no jazz musician within a thousand miles of the Himalayas, we could only assume she was exaggerating her vowels.

"Wow, you don't get that kind of service in Vegas!" Jimmy observed.

Giggling uncontrollably, she asked again, "You wan sax?" Unfamiliar with this particular part of Nepalese travel etiquette, the Americans deferred to the Indonesian who immediately spoke up, "Sure!"

"This might be my favorite place in all the world," the pilot said dreamily. Our waitress smiled, turned, and walked away. "This could get real interesting," we all agreed. Moments later our waitress returned to the table, practically salivating. Who could blame her? Before us, she placed three large plates filled to the brim with hot, mouthwatering, tantalizing, delectable *snacks!*

"Here your sax!" she said. Suddenly, I had no appetite.

I was undeterred by our misunderstanding with the waitress and emboldened by my earnings, which the money changer/chip exchanger managed to reduce from two hundred to about seventy-five dollars ("Exchange rate no good," he explained). Before we left, one of the helpers, named Rupa, perhaps the most beautiful woman I had ever laid eyes on, stopped us near the door and asked, "You want sweets?" Such dangerous questions they ask around here. Back to the Holiday Inn for these counterfeit casanovas.

I went to bed that night in the most spiritual of states—blissful but somewhat dissatisfied, oddly fulfilled but missing something. Our efforts at the Casino Royale at the Yak and Yeti had all of the elements of the quintessential spiritual experience: immersion into the unknown, mysterious beauty, risk, adventure, community in the midst of the foreign, reward (although not as we anticipated), surprise, and the ongoing issue of things getting quite lost in the translation. And, since I managed to depart with Rupa's address, there was hope too.

The next morning we set off on the Friendship Highway, a misnomer for the crater-laden, frequently washed-out, mud path between Kathmandu and Lhasa. Over the course of our Tibetan trek we employed the following modes of transportation: an air-conditioned motorcoach with high-back seating, head rests, and on-board restroom until the first washout just out of town, a large automotive object that may have been a bus at one time, turnip truck, four-wheel drive vehicle, hiking boots, and yak (my personal favorite). Truthfully, we rode the yak around in a circle for less than ten minutes. Still, it sounds much more authentic to claim to have trekked Tibet on yakback.

After an unanticipated stopover in a border town to pick up a couple of Frenchmen and leave behind six members of our party due to altitude sickness or visa difficulties, at twenty thousand feet we finally arrived at the Everest View Motel in Tingri. I'm sure that there was indeed a view of Everest somewhere, but the bitterly cold rain and dismal gray skies blocked our view. I hardly noticed the mud floor, lack of electricity, outdoor pit toilets (Note to self: Flashlight very important when traveling), or yak hair blankets that had not been cleaned since the Chinese invasion, for the pressurized pod protruding from my neck, formerly known as my head, was about to explode. If suffering is redemptive, then after that painful night, I've been redeemed. Too much in pain to stay prone, I stood outside the entire evening contemplating death or declaring a medical emergency and summoning medevac. Our guide Tenzin assured me that my headache would dissipate as we returned to altitude levels conducive to human survival. He also insisted that my body would make the necessary adjustments to acclimate to the oxygen-depleted atmosphere. "You are strong like the yak," he told me, implying that I would survive and conform to my context. Either that or he had noticed the hair growing out of my nose.

The next morning my breakfast choice of yak soup, yak butter tea, and Pabst Blue Ribbon beer was just what the doctor ordered. In Tibet this combo is now known as "the Grand Slam." Downed with a bottle of painkiller and a gallon of water, it won't alleviate the migraine, but it will cause bystanders to laugh and point for the duration of your meal. For a brief moment the rumbling in your belly and the sharp pains shooting through your abdomen will distract you from the weapons of mass destruction exploding in your sinus cavities.

The next four days gave "head-banging" a new meaning as I was tossed relentlessly into the air while the four-wheel-drive vehicle maneuvered its way along the gorge-punctured country-side. About every quarter-mile my head would get slammed up against the ceiling, providing temporary relief from the altitude-induced torment. The moon has better-maintained roadways, but no locale has friendlier natives. Over the course of our journey we learned of Tibetan customs, the history of the land and people, Buddhist practices and theology, and all about yaks.

We came to discover that the ubiquitous yak is utilized for all sorts of things. Yak meat may be prepared in a variety of ways: fried, curried, dried, and smothered. During our visit I enjoyed yak steak, yak and dumplings, yak burgers, yak pizza, yak dogs, yak and turnips, yak chili, yak meatballs and spaghetti, and yak tacos. Every yak part contributes to the betterment of society. Yak milk makes fine cheese, and yak butter fuels lamps in monasteries and provides the key ingredient in that nutritiously nauseating beverage of choice: yak butter tea. Yak wool makes for a warm blanket. Yak hide can provide a nomad with shelter from a fierce winter storm. We even heard a rumor that yak tail hair was the primary component of Father Christmas beards sold in the United States in the 1950s. Yaks are hard-working beasts of burden that serve as everything from delivery truck to snowplow. Perhaps the yak can be a lesson to those who aspire to lofty living. Even in the high places, there is no substitute for hard work, pain, and sacrifice. Or as James said in the New Testament, "Faith without works is dead." Even "jewels on the roof of the world" can end up on a necklace.

Tenzin told us about the personal relationship that families enjoy with their yaks. Each family yak is given a colorful name such as Jundrunk, Rakba, or Sida. Despite difficulty in training yaks, Tibetans recognize the great gift their partnership provides—substance, labor, and provisions. Certain nomads perform a sort of sacred tribute dance called the yak dance, labored and intense, in honor of this great creature. Tenzin also spoke reverently of the great wild yak. "Bigger than five yaks," he told me, "rarely do they go below five thousand meters." He spoke of the wild yak prowess. Once, a tour group rode in a truck up Mount Kalish to glimpse a wild yak. The wild yak saw them standing around taking snapshots with their cameras, charged their truck and single-hornedly turned it on its side. The tourists scattered, but the wild yak had made its point. Spiritual tourism is an oxymoron. To travel upward is to be prepared to pay a price. Certain truths cannot be captured on film. They are wild, elusive, and beyond belief.

There is a certain Zenlike quality to the yak's adaptation to the environment in which they not only survive, but flourish and multiply. Adjusting to the given conditions rather than fleeing to lower ground, the yak evolved to produce more red blood cells and dramatically expand its lung capacity. Its razor-sharp tongue can forage through ice, and those shaggy layers of hair keep the elements at bay. There is something to be learned from such evolutionary progress. While many of us search for a religion that can instantly bypass any obstacle we'd rather not experience, sometimes the only way around is directly through. When you find yourself at an unforeseen altitude and the elements threaten, grow your hair out, take some deep breaths, and hike another mountain or two. The spiritual life may be contraindicative of circumstance. Our preoccupied focus with alleviating our own discomfort may be nothing more than a self-obsessed search for accessible salvation. The cold, hard truth is that spiritual pilgrimage may involve a distant hike, an exploding head, or a mud-filled canyon. Adapt. Survive. Thrive. Or die.

One afternoon after finally arriving in Llasa, Jimmy and I attended a Buddhist prayer service at one of the most revered sites in all of Tibet, the Johkang Temple and Monastery, a palpably spiritual place. I watched the monks closely as they chanted the liturgies. Most participated fully in the prayers, but others gave me hope that perhaps I am not alone. There may be hope for spiritual slackers like me. One monk fell asleep and was given a sharp elbow to the upper torso by a brother. Another was definitely checking out the female pilgrims as they made the temple rounds. Another was staring off into space; one was fondling his prayer beads mindlessly, while still another was fumbling through the prayer book apparently lost and confused. You could even tell that some monks were furious when someone started an unfamiliar chant. The back row misbehaved throughout the entire service. Apparently, even in this religious tradition, it is possible to be human and holy at the same time.

Afterwards, a young monk was straightening up the prayer cushions when Jimmy approached him. "*Tashi dele*," Jimmy said, offering a Tibetan "hello" within reasonable recognition. The young monk stopped what he was doing, looked Jimmy over, smiled, and responded, "Hello, dude, you speak English?" We had found a new friend.

We had gained some unfavorable impressions of some of the monks in Llasa who seemed rude or demanding, overtly panhandling and aggressively seeking a handout from Westerners, or requiring payment for having their photograph taken. As in all religions, professions, and cultures, the few yakasses do not speak for everyone. Konchuk, our new young friend, was the real deal.

The next evening he took us to a hip little hangout frequented by young Llasaites. We talked about family and friends, girls and sports, theology and history. He told us what life was like in the monastery and shared some teachings of Buddha. We told him about what life was like in Texas, making up the horse part as we went along, and shared some teachings of Jesus. Konchuk insisted on picking up the tab for the ice cream and beer. He wanted to practice his English pronunciation on us. "*Ize krem*," he enunciated. "*Beera*," he said, adding a syllable to his Mount Everest lager.

Days later he took us out for a final traditional Tibetan meal: yak meat, potatoes, and chili paste so hot that it could ignite the entire town of Terlingua, all washed down with one final cup (thank God!) of yak butter tea. Afterward, even though it was getting late, he offered us a chance to see the inside of the monastery where the monks live, an area usually off-limits to the many pilgrims who visit Johkang.

It was almost dark as we squeezed in through a narrow wooden gate and entered an inner courtyard. We were met by the shouts of the nearby security guard: "Close! No tourist!" Konchuk said something to the guard, and he smiled and waved us on through. "What did you say to him?" we asked. "I told him," Konchuk said, "they are not tourists. They are friends." That may be the nicest thing anyone has ever said about me, that I am a friend, not a tourist.

In the inner sanctum of the monastery, the sanctity of the space permeated the atmosphere. I was reminded of a moment years earlier when I had been allowed to go beneath the Church of the Holy Sepulchre in Jerusalem where recent archaeological excavations had uncovered a portion of what may have been Calvary's Hill. Deep beneath the path that pilgrims trod for centuries, a single lamp illuminated this touchstone of salvation, an exposed foundation of a redefining moment in religious history. Small lamps also lit our way through the maze of passageways at Johkang. Finally, we arrived at Konchuk's room.

It was spartan but comfortable, possessing four furnishings: the bed, a desk, some shelves, and a water purifier. On his wall there were two posters. One displayed a red Corvette. "Do you know this car?" he asked us. "Oh yeah," we told him. The other poster pictured a scantily clad female rock star. I assumed that she was the Britney Spears of Tibet. "You know this girl?" Konchuk wondered. "No," we replied, adding, "but we'd like to." He introduced us to his uncle, a monk who shared the adjacent room. "I want you to meet my uncle," he said. Then he told his uncle, "I want you to meet my friends."

Konchuk asked if he could practice more English pronunciation before we left. His uncle mouthed the vocabulary words as Konchuk recited them, nodding and smiling in our direction. Trying my best to leave my Texas accent at home, I said with him: successive, poor, spare, population, comfort, given, kind. We pronounced many other words. The final one? Grateful. "Grateful," Konchuk enunciated clearly. "We are grateful for you," I told him, "and for this night." Konchuk gave us gifts of prayer beads and prayer scarves and walked us to the front gate. As Jimmy and I walked the streets of Llasa that night returning to our hotel, gratitude filled our hearts: gratitude for our new friend, the gifts given and received, and the experience we had shared together.

Besides the prayer beads and scarf, I returned home with several other tangible remembrances of my Tibetan trek: some splendid rugs woven by refugees, a stunning Thangka painstakingly painted by a Buddhist monk, and some simple antique boxes crafted by nomads. But one yak-related item now occupies a special place of prominence in my home. It is a happy yak, the handpainted face of a jovial beast, smiling with teeth fully exposed. The medium? Gold paint on fired mud. Mud art—now there's a valuable spiritual metaphor, for earthiness is golden. The first human, according to the Judeo-Christian tradition, was Adam. *Ad-ham* means "from the earth" or "from the ground" or "mud man." The sacred path, like the trek through Tibet, is often muddy, especially in the high places. We should feel right at home.

The flight back to Kathmandu from Llasa on China Southwest Airlines was pleasant enough, that is, if you like the taste of your own knees. We finally saw Everest. Way above the clouds, the view of such a lofty peak of pilgrimage inspires, but I am beyond that now, looking ahead to low places and a greater adventure that awaits on the ground. I salivate in anticipation, possessing an awareness and instinct for survival I hardly had before. For I now know the secret of the happy yak: mud is worth its weight in gold.

CHAPTER 24

....

Bite Me

If you bite and devour one another, take care that you are not consumed by one another.
GALATIANS 5:15

No biting. No humping. No jumping. Sorry, but those are the rules if you want to live in my house. There may be occasional exceptions or extenuating circumstances, but no one is above the law or exempt from the edicts of household decorum. No guest desires to be bitten, ridden, or jumped on, at least not before a formal introduction.

As Sam has grown older and slower, he rarely jumps on anyone anymore. Even though he will always be a horndog at heart, Sam seldom gets friendly with strangers' legs these days. And apart from the occasional puppy chomps when Sam was teething and trying out various surfaces in this strange-tasting new world, he has never tried to bite anyone—with one notable exception.

Sam relishes his role on the ministerial staff at our church. His ministry is far-reaching and profound. He serves with distinction as the official parish greeter. He has been known to howl along as the choir practices the upcoming Sunday's anthem or chase children back into their Sunday school classrooms for their own good. When grieving families gather in my office to plan a funeral service for a loved one, Sam's ministry of presence provides comfort and consolation. More than once, I have seen Sam lick the tears off the cheeks of the bereaved, place a paw on the arm of those who mourn, or even nuzzle the lap of the sorrowful. He is far more gifted and effective than I in such moments of tearfulness and woe.

One afternoon, having been cooped up inside the church office for hours with nary a newcomer to welcome, Sam and I wandered over to the grassy place between the church parking lot and the theater company next door. The church is in a developed urban area where grassy patches are few and far between. Both Sam and I realize that when nature's call comes, there had better be some nature within walking distance. Whenever Sam finds an area in which to "do the doo" (as we like to say), he typically pads around the premises for a while, enjoying the verdant landscape, sniffing and frolicking before getting down to the business at hand. This time, Sam's recreational pursuits ended abruptly as he quickly made his way back to the asphalt. I impatiently yanked him right back onto the grass as a gesture of encouragement. He moved himself right back onto the parking lot. Wondering why he didn't avail himself of the lawn-time opportunities adjacent, I reprimanded him for relieving himself on the black top just beyond the yellow striping.

We returned to the office, and I saw the reason for Sam's hesitation. In his brief encounter with the lawn, Sam had discovered a dense patch of sticker burrs. Deeply embedded in his fur, clinging to the crevices in his paws, even attached to portions of his tail, the stickers were tormenting poor Sam. Any pressure on any part of his external anatomy sent stickers deeper into his skin. "Buddy, I am so sorry," I apologized and attempted to offer comfort. He looked back at me as though I had caused this mess. "How was I to know the grass was infested with sticker burrs?" I pleaded. For the next two hours I alternated between pulling stickers out of a very resistant Sam and chasing him around the office.

Apparently the process of sticker removal was more painful than sticker infiltration. Sam's dense, curly fur had provided all sorts of places for stubborn stickers to hide, so I was forced to pull and part the hair to find those multibarbed invaders. Sam's legs and feet had always been sensitive spots, but by then a bad hip and arthritis had begun to take their painful toll. Holding his legs and paws up long enough to weed out the prickly torments caused Sam to yelp and pull back.

Sam was not pleased with the sticker pox and even less pleased with the treatment I was administering. Finally, after whimpering, whining, howling, pulling away, hiding in the corner, and trying to escape by ramming the office door, he looked right at me as if to say, "Man, I really don't want to do this, but you've given me no choice." He chomped down on the attending hand, driving four sharp prongs into my forefinger. It was a halfhearted bite to be sure, drawing no blood and piercing no epidermal layer. He immediately removed his teeth and dropped his head as if to say ashamedly, "I'm sorry." But he had made his point. There is only so much misery any creature can bear before he strikes back, even if it's "for your own good." Even if "it hurts me more than it hurts you," it still hurts.

There are a number of reasons creatures choose to chomp down. Sometimes the teeth marks are justified, which is why thoughtful folks insist on such radical concepts as "justice before peace," making sure there is right before there is might. Sometimes, the biter has been bitten too many times and is returning the favor, even if the bitee is not the original source of irritation. Inflicting pain on another may temporarily temper my own. Sometimes people are just plain mean and are in possession of concealed molars. If such tormentors cannot be defanged, they should be avoided altogether. Finally, sometimes you act like a ham sandwich and deserve to be bitten. On such occasions, you may want to pack heat, lest those around you pack mustard.

In my childhood church, several agonizing conflicts split the parish into opposing camps and created animosity among long-time friends. Since my father was in a leadership position, I learned firsthand about how even good church people could bite the hand that feeds or leads them.

When I was only twelve years old, the minister of our church, a man with a soothing voice and razor-sharp teeth, confiscated a note I had passed to a classmate. In the note I criticized church leaders for the forced resignation of a favorite youth pastor, a man not without sin, but well-loved, especially by me. The minister read this note publicly at a meeting of church leaders in an attempt to embarrass my father and force him to resign. The embarrassment and pain this man caused my father and our family was enough to cause most to lose their religion. Collectively, my family cried enough tears to provide a full-immersion baptism (the only valid kind, according to my dad). But my father stuck to his guns and his faith, did not resign, and called the pastor's bluff. Apparently, in the card game of fishy fundamentalism, a twelve-year-old's letter and one joker can't beat an honest pair and an ace in the hole. So, the preacher cashed in his chips, split the church, and got out of Dodge, leaving for a better-paying position in Dallas.

After this particular pious windbag moved on, the puncture wounds began to heal. As a congregation, we began to learn about survival, community, and an unusual concept called "love," which is apparently common in certain Christian communities. Our interim minister was an unpredictable character born in rural Tennessee. He spoke with a sort of Irish brogue speculated by many to be the result of a miraculous recovery from some sort of cancerous throat condition. Brother Harris had made a fortune as an antiques dealer in Hollywood, where, it was rumored, he had been personal friends with Pat Boone (before Boone's heavy-metal phase). After leaving Southern California, Brother Harris had devoted his life to mission work in Latin America. Since our church provided his primary support, he felt obligated to come back to the States to help us in our time of need.

A good friend, whom my dad lovingly called "the wetback" (politically incorrect, but a term of endearment I assure you), Brother Harris was fond of quoting from the New Testament epistles to remind us that the early church saw its share of conflicts as well, survived, and eventually thrived. Even in the first Christian communities people would, for some bizarre reason, "bite and devour each other," according to the Scriptures. Even back then the church tried to slay its wounded. It wasn't until they began to learn to love, accept, and support each other that they experienced true faith.

Brother Harris told us, after the infighters had left a battle-field full of flesh wounds and deeper injuries, that the church is much like a hospital. It is for those who are hurting and unhealthy. It is where we come to rest and recuperate. Our wounds are bound up, and any injury is given care. The only physician among us is Christ. The rest of us are in dire need of treatment. The church is where brokenness is bound, not caused.

In New Delhi, India, I once came upon an unexpected model for what religious communities might strive to be. I do not know much about the Jain religion, but I had heard that somewhere near the Old City next to their temple they had built and staffed a Bird Hospital. That's right: injured, wounded, or sick birds could come there or be brought in a little pushcart "Bird Ambulance" and receive free treatment and care. Apparently the Jain Bird Hospital is not a highlight on the typical tourist trail. When I attempted to tell the taxi driver where I wanted to go, he asked, "You are sick?" before inquiring "You are doctor?" but never could quite locate the place. Fortunately, I knew the general location and I spotted a bunch of birds flying overhead. I had to be close. As I approached the courtyard of the compound, Salim appeared out of nowhere. Despite my best efforts, I didn't exactly blend in with the indigenous population of New Delhi, so Salim offered to play tour guide for a small fee. I happily obliged. I was moved by what I saw there, a tangible expression of concern for the literal "least of these." We don't normally go out of our way for birds, perhaps for furry mammals more like us, but the winged rarely evoke as much empathy.

Of course, you don't normally see a priest naked either, and that's precisely what I saw standing in full view on the balcony overlooking the courtyard: the Jain priest in all his unfettered glory. I asked Salim about this peculiar religious habit. "Why is the priest naked?" Salim shrugged his shoulders and said, "Hey, I am a Muslim. We wear prayer shawls." Perhaps the priest was modeling openness and vulnerability, or maybe he was hot or couldn't afford clothes. Or maybe he was just a sicko like the rest of us. One man's flasher is another man's prophet. One man's charity is another man's dinner.

Since the hospital was part of the sacred temple compound, I was required to remove my shoes and walk barefoot among the recuperating fowl. It was equal parts touching and disgusting as I felt a variety of crunchy substances under my bare feet and noticed a large plastic bucket filled with the deceased. A variety of birds, from peacocks to parakeets, were treated here and released or returned to the wild. However, some birds had found a home here and continued to roost on the rooftop or hover nearby. The sick got cared for and the sicker go naked: sounds a lot like true religion to me.

Sometimes when I am not home, Sam will chew a hole in his rear end. The original irritant may be a flea or a mosquito bite, a skin allergy, or the nerve-racking realization that he is alone in a thunderstorm. But whatever the root cause, biting oneself or anyone else is usually a very bad idea. People get hurt. Bald spots appear. The scab still itches.

The Crusades have been over for centuries, yet some Christians are still determined to wage war on someone, anyone, even each other, in the name of Jesus. They are still hell-bent on biting and devouring one of their own. Hurtful words and harmful deeds are never signs of the Spirit. They are, more likely, evidence of the other guy. Even if you don't believe in a literal devil or the possibility of pain inflicted by red horns and a pitchfork, you know the lethal capabilities of the human mouth if you've ever been bitten, burned, or talked about badly. The devil sometimes wears a dress, a collar, or a uniform and looks all too mortal.

Over my years in the priesthood, I have learned that a degree in divinity is worthless unless accompanied by Kevlar vestments and a rabies shot. Leather-bound should describe not only your prayer book and Bible, but also your skin and self-esteem. While I make my share of mistakes and possess more than my share of shortcomings, I am probably unworthy of certain projections of evil and inadequacy that get fired my way. Once a parishioner made an appointment to see me so that he could point out in person that I am "so full of myself" that it made him sick to his stomach. Admitting that I was guilty of occupying my own skin, I asked for specific evidence of his claim. He stated that since many of my sermon illustrations were personal, I must be completely self-absorbed. I explained to him that my own stories are the only ones I can tell with any real sense of authenticity and truth. My purpose in telling them was to encourage others to embrace their own stories as occasions of God's grace in their own lives. Unconvinced, he said that I was a "liberal," apparently thinking such a label was synonymous with "sinful" or "satanic." Finally, he confessed to me that his ex-wife had had an affair with and eventually married their former minister. Many of us confuse sadness and hurt with anger and indignation. While it's no fun being an object of projection, derision, or disgust, at least I understood the source of his pain.

Recently I received an unsigned letter. One should not, as a general rule, read unsigned letters. But I needed a quick pick-me-up, being a little lonely in the midst of Sam's stay at Mom's. If one is dedicating one's life to anything even remotely worthwhile, one will occasionally receive what I have come to call "fan mail" or "love letters." They are almost always unsigned and frighteningly vindictive. One can't afford to take such criticisms personally. On the bright side, they may provide rich material for a stand-up comedy routine. This particular letter began in the following manner: "Reverend Miller, you are so pathetic." So far, we were in complete agreement. Several of my ex-girlfriends have said precisely the same thing. The letter went on to criticize my aesthetic sensibilities, policies of inclusion, and political leanings. Some day I will gather all of those unsigned letters and publish them as a single collection entitled *Teethmarks* or perhaps *Footprints on My Ass*.

The ordained ministry is a dangerous occupation. The CIA has nothing on the priesthood. Once, during the annual Blessing of the Animals at Trinity, a precious little terrier was brought forward to receive a pronouncement of God's love. Usually I refrain from placing a hand on the animal and simply make the sign of the cross over them while naming them in prayer. However, this little guy was so adorable I couldn't help but place my hand on his cute noggin as I said the blessing prayer. A nonchurchgoer, the tiny bundle of feistiness misinterpreted my friendly overtures and turned his mouth around 180 degrees to bite me. "Oh my God, I am so sorry! He's sensitive about his head," his master pointed out. The dog's name? William. Which explains everything. It turned out to be a mere flesh wound, but William's behavior perfectly illustrates the danger of the blessing business. The hand that blesses sometimes gets bitten.

Every once in a while a prophet arises among us to cut through the crap and set the spiritual record straight. Perhaps this story is apocryphal, but I hope it is true. Years ago, there was a large conference at which a number of the most prominent Baptist preachers in the United States were selected to speak. Carlyle Marney was a well-known orator and had been asked to preach the final sermon to wrap up the conference with a rousing address. Specifically, Marney was asked to listen to all of the homiletic masterpieces from that venerable pulpit and provide a spiritual summation to all that had been spoken, to reduce all of those profound and prolific discourses to a single sermon. The final moment arrived, and Marney strode to the pulpit, surveyed the rapt audience of a congregation, glanced back at the Who's Who of preachers who had preceded him, leaned forward into the microphone, and in his slow, deep southern drawl dramatically spoke a single two-syllable word. "BULLSHIT," he said, and sat back down. That might be the finest sermon ever preached.

Before I retire from the priesthood, when my pension is fully funded, I am eligible for Medicare, my bags are packed, my car is gassed and pointed in the direction of the city limits, I would like to preach one last time. I would like to assemble all of the letter-writers, slanderers, and self-appointed critics. I would hope to gather the multitude of naysayers, faultfinders, and dividers. I would want every pew packed with complainers, detractors, and backbiters. Then I would enter the pulpit, reposition my Kevlar cassock, and utter two simple, prophetic words that just might prick a callused conscience and penetrate a hardened heart, or at least make me feel better.

"Bite me," I would say, and sit down.

Now that would preach.

CHAPTER 25

············

Bugs: The Other Dark Meat

Here in Texas, we typically adhere to a strict diet. Our eating habits focus on the four major food groups: barbeque, chicken-fried steak, Tex-Mex, and beer. We like to eat, and we believe that fat is a seasoning, grease is a topping, cholesterol is a virtue, and large helpings are pleasing to God, country, and Mother. Texas is a big state so we have our share of vegetarians too, but most of them deep-fry their tofu and smother it with cream gravy. Fear not, for the fruit and vegetable world is well-represented by peach cobbler and fried okra. While Floridians can boast of the nutritional value of Gatorade, we believe a margarita with salt will replenish those same bodily fluids. And who needs antibiotics when you've got tequila?

Certain mealtime abominations, such as baked, whole wheat, or oat bran tortilla chips will not be tolerated. Real chips should make your fingers glisten and possess no nutritional value whatsoever. Real queso is made with real cheese that, if properly prepared, should leave a layer of burnt-orange natural cheese juices floating on top. To the novice, this layer resembles an oil slick and serves as a chip deterrent. However, the professional eater, aware that oil and cheese do mix, will plunge right in. A hot dog should be made of real, unmentionable animal parts, grilled over an open flame, and topped with chopped barbequed brisket, mustard, onions, and pickles. Mexican food should not be cooked with any sort of pepper whose name is not jalapeño or difficult to pronounce, and the preferred color scheme is different shades of brown. An authentic breakfast requires a six-person table for a two-person serving and is served on platters instead of plates. The biscuit should come with its own bowl of gravy, the eggs with their own bowl of chili and salsa. Grits may be consumed with butter, sugar, or Tabasco. The breakfast restaurant should be owned by a police officer, and he should use only his grandmother's recipes. While we would never go so far as to eat barbequed lard, we would seriously consider it and wonder whether it could be battered and fried.

A friend of mine recently moved from Texas to the beautiful state of Colorado. He has a lovely mountain view from his back deck, skis in the winter, and does not swelter in the summer. Of Texas he reminisces, "I miss the food and the people, in that order." Since moving, he's lost ten pounds and bought some Birkenstocks. I am worried about him, but I am certain that his condition is nothing that a good therapist and a basic truck-stop cafe couldn't cure.

The first time I saw Sam eat a bug I stood aghast. It is not that I have room to talk when it comes to eating habits, but Sam did not even slow down to sniff, rip off a bit, or pick at it to see if it would taste good. As soon as the winged insect landed, Sam made a beeline in its direction and caught it between his teeth. Unlike some of the other unlikely food candidates that hardly touch the sides of Sam's mouth, sliding directly towards gastrointestinal bliss, Sam actually chewed this insect, apparently savoring every mouthwatering morsel. The cold, hard, crunchy truth is that Sam likes to eat bugs and will do so at every opportunity. Though he is partial to the aerial variety, he will sometimes settle for a grasshopper or even a roach. But who am I to judge another for his eating habits? One man's pest is another man's nacho; one creature's vermin is another's veal. Besides, Sam's high protein orientation may turn out to be better for his long-term well-being than grain-based diets advocated by certain dieticians. According to Sam, mites make right. A beetle a day keeps the doctor away. Got moths? Weevils—it's what's for dinner. You want fries with those flies?

While I do not find Sam's culinary preferences all that appetizing, they call to mind the nature of God's providence. Blessing, bounty, and abundance are significant issues for our bellies as well as our souls. Weighty theological choices such as variety, taste, and options pertain to spiritual health as well as individual taste buds. For those who hunger and thirst after righteousness, spiritual sustenance, *and* a full tummy, it is important to ask these culinary questions: "What's there to eat around here? Who's hungry?" And finally, "Are you gonna eat that?"

God will provide. However, God may not provide what we demand, expect, or think we need. When the children of Israel were wandering in the wilderness complaining and longing for "the fleshpots of Egypt" despite their miraculous deliverance from bondage, the Lord provided for their nutritional needs with quail and manna. The quail were difficult enough, more bones than bird, and capable of flying right off your plate. But the manna— now that takes some culinary creativity! Can you imagine the first person to suggest ingesting that stuff growing on the rocks? "Hey, let's scoop these crusty white particles off these rocks and make some pancakes!" Syrup anyone?

In the spiritual realm, we tend to be finicky eaters and stick with what we know. Auntie Mame's timeless observation that "Life is a banquet, and most poor suckers are starving to death!" is just as true in the religious world. A steady diet of the all too familiar might make us feel full, but it certainly isn't very interesting, and creates large communities of meatheads. Vary the menu! Be daring in your selections. Try new things. Eat more slowly. God has provided spiritual sustenance in the most unlikely places, from the most unlikely sources. Grazing is permitted. Taste and see that the Lord is good—not always good for you, but consistently good.

Remember that tastes are a matter of individual preference, not cause to take up arms or start new religions. Most conflicts, disagreements, and even wars in the name of religion have more to do with matters of style than substance. As a parish priest, I've seen parishioners nearly come to blows over such significant issues as flower arrangements, hymn selections, and how to stuff a turkey. What is yucky to one person might be yummy to another. What someone finds sacrilegious may be sanctifying to someone else. That which is downright sinful to a particular seeker may be the direct path to salvation for another. Judge not, and be not judged. Just because you don't desire a serving of worm casserole doesn't mean you shouldn't pass it on around the table.

The implications of abundance, bounty, and blessing also suggest that we become aware of those who go without. The true test of one's spirituality, the ultimate question in this life is, as Martin Luther King Jr. expressed it, "What are you doing for others?" Feeding people is always a sacramental act. At my home parish we are blessed with a genuine appreciation for beauty and the arts. We place high value on the spiritual significance of architecture, artwork, stained glass, gardens, and music. But we also believe strongly in the sacramental significance of bologna sandwiches, bacon and eggs, and buttermilk biscuits. Six days a week a homeless person or anyone with an appetite can find a meal there. We spend a lot of money on food, and those are funds well-spent.

Often, when I sit down to a delicious meal and begin to chow down, Sam will come and sit right beside me. While I'm eating, he will put his face close to mine and mimic my jaw movements, acting out the mastication of every morsel. His entire head will follow my fork from plate to mouth, and his intense stares at my entrée unmistakably indicate that he is wondering if I'm going to finish all that all by myself. Sam's bugging me is obnoxious but endearing and reminds me that mine is not the only mouth to feed in my self-absorbed world.

In God's world, there is plenty for everyone, if all of us are willing to share. The Creator has provided a smorgasbord of edible delights. Whether you are partial to barbeque or bugs, tofu or teriyaki, acorns or ants, the creation teems with tasty treats. Some are good for you. All are good. So pass the plate and eat up.

But save some for Sam.

CHAPTER 26

....

El Toro

Sam lost his manhood just before testicular reasoning, a sometimes fatal condition that affects males from age nine to ninety, set in. While the loss of his *cojones* calmed him down a notch or two, it did not seem to diminish his attraction to the poodle down the street. In fact, the only times I've seen Sam overtly agitated were when Ally saunters in front of our house, purposefully shaking her thing in his direction. Sam, a dog of few woofs, will howl, yelp, bark, shift his weight from paw to paw, stand on his hind legs, claw the window, dance around in circles, douse himself with cold water, and read the entire genealogical section of the Gospel of Matthew in an attempt to decrease the sexual tension and preserve his sanity. Should a Barry White tune be playing in the background, Sam refuses to be held accountable for the living room furniture or any human leg within humping distance. While food and sleep rate slightly ahead of romance and despite the fact that his plumbing has been disconnected and the well sealed off, Sam is still looking for love.

Aren't we all? Isn't there something inherent in our being that seeks intimacy, mutuality, and relationship? Even if such deeper connections are not forthcoming, who among us hasn't gotten worked up over the possibility of a little hormonal dialogue?

In matters of the heart as in life, some are more successful than others. For example, my parents were married for forty-seven years. While they would be quick to admit that it wasn't all harmony, happiness, and bliss, there is something to be said for longevity. To think that it almost never came to pass! If not for my father's *Testoronic* fortitude (a word I made up combining *Toro* with testosterone), my mother would have married a tall, blonde, wealthy German guy whose family owned the big department store in town. In fact, she was virtually promised to this fellow when my father swooped in like Zorro and swashbuckled his way into her heart. I have seen my mother's high school yearbook senior picture, and I can say with certitude that she was a looker, one hot commodity. However, I also read directly under her photo that her extracurricular activities consisted of being the flag girl in the band and that collecting pennies was her hobby. So let's just say that, like Sam, my mom was quite adept at getting by on her looks.

When pressed for more details about why she dumped the German in favor of my much poorer and far less sophisticated father, my mother confessed, "Well, he was really cute." Thank God for shallowness, or I wouldn't be here.

My father had laid down the wedding gauntlet. "Come, go with me to the Justice of the Peace and let's get married right now, or adios, *Señorita!*" They were married that afternoon. "Yessir, back then they called me 'El Toro,'" my father would brag. He maintained this image to the very end. Once while in the hospital near death, his blood pressure spiked. The doctor asked him if he had "white coat syndrome," the condition in which blood pressure rate increases temporarily at the sight of a physician. My father told the doctor, "No sir, but I've got short skirt syndrome: as long as I can see that nurse, parts of me shall remain elevated." Long live the bull.

Most of my married friends are quite content to have found a life partner. Still, they press me for information about my dating life, for a sort of vicarious thrill, I suppose, for those who have traded the chaos and unpredictability of the range for the comfort and stability of the barn. "I want details," my male friends will insist. "Don't leave out anything," as if my nightly exploits were suitable for the Spice Channel. The cold, limp truth is that Disney would be bored by my love life. Animal Planet, or even the Golf Channel, is far more titillating. Okay, maybe not the Golf Channel.

Oh sure, there was the Brazilian goddess who nicknamed me *El Gato* one summer in Rio, apparently quite a compliment in that culture. And yeah, there was the swimsuit model and her ballerina friend, but that was a long time ago when I actually had something in common with nineteen-year-olds. I do remember my rendezvous with the lovely French-Canadian dancer from Montreal. Acknowledging my Lone Star heritage, she showed up at the airport in Chicago wearing a clingy mini-dress with cowboy boots, yelling "yeehah" in my direction, waving one hand at me, and holding White Sox tickets in the other. The cab driver found it unbelievable that I would dare inquire as to who they were playing.

Perhaps this is the stuff that dreams are made of, since they most certainly are dreams. The reality is much less inspiring. My night prowls could put an insomniac to sleep. It's not so much a jungle out there as it is a petting zoo with very tame, if not stuffed, animals. The call of the wild is, in actuality, a depressed sigh. Personal examples abound.

Once I was standing at a bar in Austin, waiting for the country-reggae band to begin. You can actually hear such hybrid sounds in Austin—God bless Texas! I wear a silver ring with a cross etched into it on the ring finger of my right hand; it was a gift from a group of students long ago. I rarely leave home without it, and that night was no exception. As I stood there sipping a Shiner Bock, a very attractive blonde woman bellied right on up to the bar beside me and stood very close, invading my personal space. She looked into my eyes, smiled, and coyly inquired, "You don't remember me, do you?" While a lot could have changed in the twenty-five years since her baptism, I could not have officiated, since I would've been in kindergarten at the time. Since I was absolutely positive that I did not remember her, because I had never ever met her, seen her, or even heard of her, I told her the truth and said, "No."

Undeterred, she grabbed my right hand, gazed in a sort of devotional way at my cross ring, turned it round and round in a seductive if not sacrilegious manner, licked her lips, and asked point-blank, "Are you Catholic?"

"Episcopal," I replied, not wanting to elaborate or waste any words that might come back to haunt me.

Her eyes narrowed and her mouth broadened as if recognizing some significant spiritual connection, and she said, "Oh yeah, there's that guy who was on *Saturday Night Live*. Joe *Piscopo*." I always attract the smart ones.

Then there was the slicker-than-celluloid news anchorwoman, still known to my friends as "the mass of neuroses." She was new to Texas, stunning on and off camera, and truly museum-quality (you can look but if you touch, alarms will go off and you will be arrested). I tried to help her assimilate into our strange culture by buying her a Willie Nelson doll in Luckenbach and renaming her prissy white dog "Flaco Jimenez" after the great Texas Tejano musician. She got neither. After a series of formal dates had earned me exactly one dry peck on the cheek, I decided to make my move.

We had been invited to an intimate dinner party hosted by Lady Bird Johnson honoring a well-known ambassador and his wife in the private dining room of the LBJ library and museum. My date was very impressed by being in the company of a room full of powerful folks. After a lovely evening of stimulating conversation, impeccable service, and extraordinary camaraderie, things began to wind down. Right next to the dining room was an exact replica of the Oval Office during Johnson's tenure as president. I figured if it worked for JFK and Clinton, surely it could work for me. As my Bible teachers always told me, "Context is everything!" On our way to the elevator I invited her to detour into the chief executive's inner sanctum, assuming a first kiss in the Oval Office would be memorable, romantic, and might even lead to other presidential maneuvers. I could envision it clearly. "Hail to the Chief" would be our song. Pretending to call attention to Lincoln's nose on a portrait hanging in a hidden corner of the room, I attempted to plant one on her lips. I missed. She ducked out of my way, darted out the door, and ran for the nearest Secret Service agent. The elevator ride down was tense as the ambassador and his wife exchanged awkward pleasantries with the flustered priest and his elusive date. I felt about as desirable as Richard

Nixon after Watergate and as smooth as Spiro Agnew articulating a foreign policy. At that moment, I was to love what Dan Quayle is to spelling bees. Maybe I just need to watch less TV; that or perhaps go for the Fox News girls next time. I hear they know how to party.

Oh, and how can I forget the Southern California cutie I met in Florence, Italy? A momentary conversation at an outdoor café led to a nine-month long-distance fling, "relationship" being much too serious a word. She seemed to have everything going for her, or at least an impressive trifecta of matchmaking criteria. She was gorgeous, she lived on the beach, and her family owned a jet. The great thing about a long-distance romance is that every time you see each other, it is like being on vacation. The daily grind of my ongoing routine was interrupted at key intervals by a hottie girl who could afford to pay for both of our cheeseburgers, her meal of choice. What's not to love? But eventually conversation was inevitable. It's amazing what one discovers by actually talking to another person. For example, that they have absolutely *nothing* to say! Once, seeking to describe a character flaw I am not too fond of in other people, I used the word "superficial" in a sentence. Although she frequently did not respond when I attempted verbal communication, she sensed that this word might be fairly significant. Not wanting to admit that she did not know the definition of the word, nor how to use a dictionary, she asked me, "So, what's the *full* meaning of 'superficial'?" Similar to the *full* capacity of "vacuous," I believe. Shortly thereafter she started dating a guy who smoked a lot of dope and jumped out of an airplane for a living. I moved quickly into my librarian phase.

Don't get me wrong. I have had meaningful relationships with a multitude of wonderful, intelligent, articulate, spiritual, talented, kind women. Most were smarter and more capable than I; their only character flaw was choosing to date me. We genuinely connected on many profound levels: intellectually, philosophically, theologically. My failures in love are primarily because of my own unreasonable expectation that the "girls are always greener" on the other side, (Note to Emanuela Columbo in Italy: call me if you don't marry Mario!) The usual suspects play a role in my bachelorhood: fear of commitment, failure to integrate masculine and feminine selves, family of origin issues, unresolved oedipal tensions, unwillingness to bond with cats, sudden inability to speak English upon hearing the question, "So where is this relationship headed?" a personal preference for wearing "tighty whities" until they are neither. Or it could be that it's just taken me a long time to figure out that one being cannot meet all of my needs.

According to an ancient African proverb, it takes an entire village to raise a man who is not full of bull: drinking buddies, family and friends, dogs, an employer, God, and a girlfriend. As I grow wiser and more seasoned in the ways of love, I am beginning to heed my friends' caring advice: to quit picking dates like I pick my fruit, barely ripe and right off the vine. As a buddy once implored, "Quit dating girls with puppy breath." Meanwhile, I still believe in the sacrament of marriage, and I am reasonably certain that my serial monogamy will some day cease. Uma Thurman is still available, right? Love may be strange, cruel, intense, painful, disappointing, fulfilling, and exhilarating, but one thing is certain. It is a potent, powerful force to be reckoned with. It cannot be denied, and it will not forsake us, regardless of our age, sex, species, orientation, or even if we've lost certain key anatomical components. A little bit can go a long way.

Thelma was pushing eighty years old when I met her. Every Wednesday morning I took communion to her at the nursing home where she resided in south Austin. She was a longtime member of my congregation; her husband had died years before, and she was in poor health. She was also strong and determined, having survived bypass surgery the previous year. Often when I would visit, Thelma didn't have the strength to sit up, much less get out of bed. Before I would administer the Holy Sacrament I would typically ask if I could say "a little prayer" for her. "Please— oh, I need it," would be her consistent response. I'd take her hand, and we'd pray together. Then, after a brief visit discussing nieces, grandkids, nephews, and various tidbits of neighborhood, nursing home, and church gossip, we'd share the Lord's Supper, and I'd be on my way. I always looked forward to my visits with Thelma. She often had a loving look in her eyes and seemed genuinely happy to see me.

Months passed. Even a few years. Thelma got better and had begun to sit up in her wheelchair, fully primped by the time I arrived. One day Thelma was completely dolled up, wearing a special pink velour jogging suit and a gold cross necklace. She wore her glasses and her teeth were firmly in place. She had brushed her hair and the room smelled like perfume. Thelma's custom was to gaze at me intently during our visits. But this time she was being overwhelmingly flirtatious, looking up just long enough to cast coquettish glances in my direction. We had our little prayer together, and Thelma wondered if she could ask me a little question. "Of course you can, Thelma," I told her. Finally summoning the courage to look deeply into my eyes, she asked, "Will you marry me? I love you, Bill." With love, as in prayer, a little goes a long way.

I smiled and told her how flattered I was that she would think so highly of me, but that I was her priest so I wouldn't be able to marry her. I told her how much I loved and cared for her also, as her priest, and how much our visits meant to me. Finally I told her that my girlfriend might have a problem with it. Thank you very much, Thelma, for thinking such wonderful thoughts about me, but I would have to graciously decline and continue to be your priest rather than your husband.

At a very deep level I was touched by Thelma's overture. Her tenacity was further proof of the power of this basic life force. Our visits continued and they were mostly pleasant, although occasionally uncomfortable. Once, she accused me of thinking she was "old and ugly." My father, upon hearing her story, asked insensitively if she "had much money." Once a Toro, always a Toro. When Thelma died, her daughter presented me with a small stuffed bunny she was quite fond of. Thelma had named this animal "Bill Baby" and slept with it every night. I kept it on a shelf in my office for years, right next to the section on theology. Redemption. Sanctification. Salvation. Bill Baby. It spoke volumes.

One does not have to fully understand something to believe in it, even to believe strongly and unequivocallly. Love, indeed, may be elusive, but it is most assuredly present. The apostle was right. Love hopes all things, believes all things, and endures all things. Sentimentality, melodrama, and niceness shall all pass away, but love will last. Love never fails.

I believe that one day *El Toro* will trade in chasing red fabric for a more committed life of interdependence and reciprocity. Until such time, however, you might want to get out of the way and take refuge in the barn. The range can be a dangerous place.

CHAPTER 27

....

Let Sleeping Dogs Pray

Regarding the town of Shigatse, the Tibetan guidebook forewarns, "Keep a watchful eye out for dogs—have plenty of stones at your disposal. For a good night's sleep, ear plugs are strongly recommended." Shigatse is known for its omnipresent packs of stray dogs that roam the streets, threaten the populace, and disturb the peace from dusk till dawn. In the wee hours especially, one can expect to hear howling courtesy of the canine gangs. If it is peace and quiet you are after, keep moving. There is no rest for the weary in Shigatse.

Given the city's reputation for canine chaos, I was surprised to discover the most docile dogs I have ever encountered at the Tashihunpo Monastery. So mellow, laid-back, and peaceful were they that I theorized that someone had drugged their dog food with chicken-flavored valium or baked a little ganja into their dog biscuits. I have met stuffed animals far more menacing than these guys. Lounging around the monastery grounds, these pups had discovered the secret to stress-free living. They were so calm and content that their very presence exuded a sort of serene tranquility apparent to everyone within petting distance. Watching them was the wellness equivalent of a fistful of medication, a yoga class, a basket of fruit, and an afternoon of reading at the beach with tropical beverages provided free of charge.

How did the monastery dogs became so different from the thugs outside of the gates? Tenzin, the guide for our Tibetan trek, explained that it had nothing to do with moral superiority, spiritual susceptibility, or intellectual capability. It had much to do with being at the right place at the right time, or at least a better place for a longer duration of time. Add a little positive karma to the mix, and the monks had a bunch of holy hounds on their hands.

As Tenzin described the process of transformation, he combined his storytelling stylings with a little theological discourse. The first lesson relates to power and prestige, often the antithesis of a lifestyle of contemplation and communion with the Divine. If a dog is famous or important, Tenzin suggested, he will rarely end up at the monastery. Rather, an assortment of difficult life circumstances will lead a dog to a life of prayer. Perhaps the dog is critically ill, or the owner is in dire economic straits and cannot afford to feed the animal. Many monastery residents were former street dogs who had nowhere else to go and somehow found enough religion to lead them to Tashihunpo. The kind monks open their doors to all of these animals. Turning no dog away, they feed and care for all who apply for admission. The dogs find their way to the monastery like many of us find our way to God— an approach of last resorts, when desperate times call for desperate measures, even prayer.

But Tenzin acknowledged that the dogs arrive at the monastery "mostly by karma." Lesson two reflects this reality, that even in the nonhuman realm, what goes around comes around. Tenzin illustrated the karma connection using an ancient Tibetan tale of how the clever, tricky cat became an indoors animal while the patient, honest dog was banished to keep guard on the outside.

One day the prized silver bowl belonging to the Master came up missing, pilfered from its locked case. The Master was very distraught and agonized over its loss.

Dog said to Cat, "We must find our Master's bowl."

But Cat replied, "It's not my bowl. I have all that I need in the way of such creaturely comforts. The bowl makes no difference to me. If you want to try to find it, go get it without me."

Then, one day Dog spotted the thieves who had made off with the bowl. Again he begged of Cat to participate in the retrieval, but Cat's response was the same song, second verse. So Dog bit Cat and insisted, "Come with me."

Cat went along so as not to be bitten again. Eventually they found the stolen bowl, took it back, and set off for home. When they arrived at the river, Cat persuaded Dog to carry him on his back. Agreeing, Dog swam against the current while Cat held the bowl. Cat promised to give the bowl back to Dog as soon as they arrived on the other side. Of course, immediately upon reaching the shore, Cat scampered off and made a formal feline presentation of the bowl to Master, claiming that Dog was out roaming the streets up to no good. Master was well-pleased with Cat and called him "beautiful and good."

When Dog finally arrived, soggy and out of breath, Master scolded him saying, "All you ever do is eat and sleep, and look! Why can't you be like Cat?" He then tied Dog to an outdoor post and banished him to the exterior forever. Cat would dwell inside the house with Master. Cat smiled. Dog cried.

Tenzin explained that karma eventually caught up with Dog and Cat alike. Therefore, Dog, whose motives were pure and trustworthy, is the highest animal, first in the animal line to be reincarnated as a human being. Cat is way down on the list, somewhere between the hyena and the possum. Thanks to karma, tricky and clever will only get you so far for so long. Eventually your true motives will determine your ultimate destruction or elevation. We reap what we sow. Karma keeps tabs on such things.

Tenzin elaborated on how these dogs are transformed at the monastery from supreme scoundrels to serene saints. A sort of spiritual osmosis takes place. By surrounding themselves with spiritual pursuits and compassionate persons, the dogs in time acquire similar dispositions. Their souls begin to reflect the wisdom of their environment, and their personalities appropriate the piety of their setting. Night and day, the dogs hear the chants, readings, and prayers uttered by the monks. Thus, they receive the same blessing as the humans who worship unceasingly. The dogs become "like monks," Tenzin said. The monastery dogs, awake and asleep, are immersed in prayer. Such a spirituality soaks in, elevating their spirits so that in the next life they will progress to become fully human. The dogs outside the monastery do not receive the benefits of the blessing, because they are too busy howling to hear the sweet strains of praise, too busy fighting and worrying to benefit from the peaceful milieu. For life on the street is filled with strife and stress. The outside dogs wander aimlessly all night long, while the sleeping monastery dogs pray without ceasing, at rest and in peace.

The third lesson relates to the baggage we keep, the places we frequent, and the causes we contemplate. Spirituality, sense, and consciousness have something in common: location, location, location! While we are born with particular talents and certain predispositions, environmental factors can transform our souls,

increase our faith, and contribute to karma. The locations where
we take our naps and meals, where we find our friends and com-
rades, where we place our values and our priorities determine
whether we find ultimate peace or whether our attempts at tranquility are repeatedly disturbed. Sometimes our spiritual state has
more to do with physical placement than proper perspective, and
the former can effectively alter the latter.

Sam has two favorite spaces that consistently revive and refresh
him. Often in his solitude, Sam will seek out a cool, smooth surface to sprawl out upon and enjoy a deep slumber. Although carpet
may be available in the next room, and the soft, warm, cushioned
places may provide more comfort and security, there is nothing
like cold tile or even chilly bathroom porcelain to revive the soul
and rejuvenate the spirit.

Nothing that is, except the wind. Sam will sometimes wander
outside and thrust his head toward the heavens simply to feel the
wind blow on his face. A wonderful "Far Side" comic depicts a dog
whose head is protruding from a car window, enjoying the breeze
blowing directly on his face. As other cars pass by, he notices the
humans sitting inside and asks, "Why don't they stick their heads
out of the window?" Such a valid question. Why don't we stick our
heads out of the window or crane our necks to sense the currents
of air that may revive us? Sam never misses an opportunity to stick
his head out of the window of my truck. And should the window
be up, he will place his nose directly in front of the air conditioning vent, achieving the same effect while riding shotgun.

Lesson three teaches us that holy spaces surround us. Quiet,
cool, wind-blown, spirit-filled places. Whether we place ourselves
there may mean the difference between sighs of satisfaction and
howls of unrest, between spiritual tranquility and pangs of distress.

The fourth lesson learned from the monastery dogs relates to
the purpose and nature of prayer. Prayer might, in fact, change
things, but more importantly, prayer changes us. Prayer is not just
an opportunity to get more dog biscuits or have a few more bones
diverted in my direction. Prayer is not simply the compilation of
a to-do list that we present succinctly to the Great Errand-Runner
in the Sky. It is a poor excuse for prayer that recites a litany of personal needs to God and then sits back and waits for God to attend

to them. Instead, prayer is an ever-expanding state of awareness of God's presence, a posture of receptivity, an appreciation for the opportunity of being so close. It is an offering of praise and adoration. It is a sleepy, sprawling, prostrate position that faces up, down, and all around, as it dreams, wanders, and imagines. Prayer is that place where cool, smooth surfaces press up against our cheeks, where the wind blows freely when it will, and we are satisfied simply to feel it on our faces.

Sometimes I tease Sam whenever he wanders off to get prone and get another nap, remarking that he'd better get plenty of sleep so he'll be well-rested enough to go to bed early. But Sam and the monastery dogs are well aware that sometimes the most enlightened option is not to act or react. But just to be. Aware. Asleep. Appreciative. Sometimes the best advice for the stressed-out soul is this: *Don't* just do something. Stand there. Better yet, lie there. And pray.

CHAPTER 28

. . . .

Turtle Time

For lo, the winter is past;
The rain is over and gone;
The flowers appear on the earth;
The time of the singing of birds is come;
And the voice of the turtle is heard in the land.
SONG OF SOLOMON 2:11-12 (SORT OF)

Whether the "turtle" referred to above is an old-fashioned rendering of love-bird or a highly hilarious misquote, I find it provocative. This quote comes from a book on spiritual discipline I've been reading lately. I had decided it was time to get serious about my lack of prayer and quiet time and add some non-negotiable routine to the chaos of my life. There I was, sitting up straight in my special revelatory chair in the loft, that higher space reserved for religious reading, sober thoughts, and the finer arts such as Destroyer and karaoke, looking all pious and upright, thinking pure thoughts related to nuns, reading profound points about sacred awareness, when the turtle quote poked me like an errant flipper. I hooted so loud that Jack raced upstairs, and Sam actually opened one eyelid.

The words represent a portion of a poetic passage from the Song of Solomon. During services of Holy Matrimony, this reading ranks second in popularity, just behind I Corinthians 13, the "Love" chapter, or as I call it, "The Barry White Chapter." "Darling, if I speak in the tongues of men and of angels but have not love, I am but a noisy gong. Oh baby, if I have the power to move mountains but have not love, I am but an impotent fool."

The idyllic lyric of Solomon's song takes it way back beyond Marvin Gaye and speaks to the time when true love ushers in a romantic and sensual paradise. Rainbows appear. Flowers blossom. Waves whisper sweet nothings gently on the beach. It's like Hawaii without the ukuleles. Then, to summarize this charmed encounter between two tender souls, the voice of the delicate bird known as the turtledove serenades the lovers, wooing them into enchanted bliss, cooing them on toward eternal happiness. Only in the above version, the crescendo flattens as the aberrant warbling of a hard-shell tortoise, the indelicate honks of a horny-beaked land reptile, sound the alarm. When the unlikely voice of the turtle is heard in the land, the bird-crossed lovers must figure it's time to resubscribe to match.com. The honeymoon is over. Somebody paved Paradise and knocked down the nest. It's time to pull their heads out of the cuddly love shell and get back into the water.

Then again, having never had a significant conversation with a turtle, I write from a place of unknowing. Since I have never actually heard the voice of a turtle, I must allow that such vocalizing could be as seductive as a Barry White ballad. My assumptions may belie my mammalistic ignorance. It is also possible that "turtle" is simply an archaic reference to "turtledove," two-syllable shorthand for lovey-dovey. Not knowing the author's intent or the turtle's ability to hit a low C, and possessing little background in either Solomonic imagery or reptilian range, I admit to the possibility that I do not know what I am talking about. If the turtle wants to sing a love song, who am I to turn down the volume? Let the turtle's voice be heard in all the land! Ladies and gentlemen, it's turtle time!

Some people dive with sharks. I swim with turtles. Although this behavior may not elevate my eligibility status in the dating pool, it made for an interesting day at the beach. After last summer's strict regimen of writing and a month of absolutely no partying except on religious holidays or days ending in y, I was ready to kick back and relax at a little dilapidated surfer cottage on Sunset Beach, the north shore of Oahu. The Realtor had described it as "rustic." My companion on this surfing safari, Everett McKinley, used a more subtle real estate term: "shithole." We spent most of our dozen days away from Honolulu, having just missed the errant surfboard's breaking of Cameron Diaz's nose in Waikiki by a day. Had my longboard been involved in the mishap, perhaps it would have led to some beautiful Solomonic poetry between us, or at the very least, I could've laid hands on her and prayed for her healing.

I was profoundly affected by my time in Oahu, suggesting minor changes to the eucharistic liturgy on my first Sunday back at Trinity Church:

Celebrant: The Lord be with you, dudes!
People: Dude! And also with you!

Having discovered the Hawaiian word for "priest" and recognizing my sacred duty as the head priest of my parish, I implored my flock to start calling me "Big Kahuna." These liturgical innovations were never embraced by my people, even on Hawaiian Shirt Sunday. Go figure.

We met some delightful folks in Paradise, including a teacher of comparative religion, a Californian chiropractor, an assortment of psycho-hotties, and even big-wave legend Ken Bradshaw, a fellow Houstonian who learned to surf on the Texas Gulf Coast. Our constant companions in the surf turned out to be *honu*, Hawaiian sea turtles. These beautifully goofy creatures were everywhere. We even got into an up-and-down rhythm with these wide-board bobbers. They'd come up for air just as I was going down to drown. Their breaths, however, were far less frequent than my falls. One day, we paid a special visit to a favorite hangout of the sea turtles, a small beach inlet nicknamed Turtle Cove. There I learned some things about turtles, timing, and the true mission of humanity: to save us from ourselves and each other.

Basking for Jesus

The basking Hawaiian Sea Turtles will crawl out on to the sand to bask and rest mainly during the daylight hours.
—A SIGN IN TURTLE COVE, OAHU

I have never understood Sam's preference for cool, hard places. Lying prone on a solid surface would provide little comfort to my bones. Wouldn't it be more comfortable to snuggle under some down-filled blanket or assume the fetal position in a cuddly, warm, soft spot? Sam demonstrates an overwhelming preference for the opposite. His favorite resting position in all the world is wrapped around the bottom of the toilet. He is so enamored of the "porcelain position" that he will not budge for the loudest of flushes. Sometimes I am annoyed by Sam's consistent nonmovement and his choice of resting place. I don't get it. Doesn't he know the purpose of that water-filled fixture in that particular room? Isn't he aware that his only reason for being is to keep me constantly entertained? What a basker!

One of my favorite cartoons features a minister sitting in his study engaged in quiet time and prayer. The computer is off. The books are closed. The writing tablet is put away. The parish secretary barges in, seeing what he is not doing, and observes, "Oh, glad to see I'm not interrupting anything important!" We tend to devalue the static side of spirituality, but the spiritual life is not about engaging in the greatest amount of religious activity. Sometimes, the most profound response is not to respond. Finding our way can be about finding the cool and unusual spaces that refresh us. While organized religion may not place the highest value on stillness and rest, personal spirituality certainly does. When the sea turtles would lie in the sun and simply bask, some onlookers would become impatient and unhappy. *Don't just lie there, do something!* they seemed to be thinking. Basking on a beach, sitting in a study, resting on a rock, even hugging a piece of porcelain—all are part of the holy process of renewal. It's okay to engage in such behavior. Even during daylight hours. Even if everyone else is quite ready to go.

Isn't That Special?

This basking is a natural behavior special to Hawaiian Sea Turtles.
—A SIGN AT TURTLE COVE, OAHU

Why are we often threatened by the natural behavior of others? Is it because we remain out of our own elements, oblivious to the divinity within us and throughout all creation? Out of tune and out of touch with our particular purpose and place? In Hawaii, Everett and I slipped into a natural groove wholly dependent on our mellow milieu. There was no nightlife on the north shore, so there were no late nights. There was no air conditioning, so our bodies acclimated and felt quite comfortable. There was no television, computer, or telephone. The glory of God and beauty of the world provided sufficient inspiration. Our environment, which we fully engaged, consisted of the sun, sea, waves, beach, stars, moon, and wind. We ate fresh tuna and ripe pineapple, and drank an occasional mai-tai. There was no health club, but we felt healthier than ever. Awakened by the sun, drawing inspiration from the stars, gaining strength from the sand, achieving balance on the waves, we were empowered by powers available to all. When we got tired, we basked and rested on the beach. That behavior came naturally, too. It was a blissful, natural rhythm where we lived out St. Irenaeus's maxim, "The glory of God is the human being fully alive!"

Much unhappiness in life arises from our inability to revere creation and acknowledge our elemental selves. As a result, we prevent others from enjoying their stretch of the sand. At the beach, a mother yelled at her toddler son, "Stay out of the sand!" We set ourselves and others up for failure. We run aground morally when we deny the truth about ourselves and our surroundings. Our ethical schizophrenia may derive from our attempts to walk the beach without getting sand in our toes, to tell the *honu* to wake up and quit wasting everybody's time, to deny what comes naturally to others as downright sinful. One creature's comfort is another's line drawn in the sand, but the beach is big enough for all of us.

If It Ain't Broke

Please Do Not Touch the Turtles
—A SIGN IN TURTLE COVE, OAHU

The signs were very clear about giving the honu space to live, breathe, bask, and be. The warnings were explicit enough to deter the most determined do-gooder. "It is illegal to disturb the turtles in the ocean or on the beach, and fines can be imposed for doing so. If you see a green turtle basking or sleeping ashore, leave it alone."

Keeping a respectful distance and letting others be does not come easily for some of us. We watched incredulously as a dangerous man with a towel and his evil, sidekick girlfriend possessing a lethal bottle of water proceeded to ruin a perfectly good day at the beach for a particular turtle, which was trying to bask and rest. I am not saying that this guy was from Jersey, but there were clues. Nets jersey. Gold jewelry. Chest hair. Loud girlfriend. The dangerous man began his assault by getting in the turtle's face and wiping down the turtle's head with a beach towel reeking of sunscreen.

"Did you see him trying to get the sand out of his eyes with his flipper?" the guy explained, obviously an authority on Hawaiian sea turtle behavior. Assuming that these shell-shocked waterboys have been beaching themselves for several millennia, don't you think they might be familiar with the concept of sand? For a creature whose natural behavior is to embed himself in a sandy beach, sand is not the enemy. Morons with towels are!

Concerned citizen number-one proceeded to sculpt the sand into a massive eyebrow protruding from the turtle's head, but his brilliant girlfriend would not be outdone in kindness. She walked over to the turtle and poured an entire bottle of Evian on top of its head, explaining, "There! That should help! All he needed was some fresh water!" Let us ponder the logic of this particular bikini-clad marine biologist for a moment. A *sea* turtle lives in the *sea*, and last time I checked, the *sea* is composed entirely of *salt water*. *Salt water* is the natural element of choice, the preferred context for the *sea* turtle. Though a human might prefer to drink or bathe in fresh water, the sea turtle prefers *sea* water. I am relatively certain that I heard the turtle's voice throughout the land, screaming, "Who is pouring acid on my head?!" The sea turtle immediately got up and headed straight toward the ocean, hurried if not harmed, by the thoughtful deeds of those just trying to help.

Whenever an individual or a group comes to me with the words, "Some of us are concerned," I know that I'm in for trouble. That's typically code for "We are so screwed up that we must immediately project onto someone else!" Our efforts to fix, change, help, correct, or save others, assuming that we know what's best for them, are incredibly dangerous. Our missionary efforts are typically little more than matters of personal hygiene, based on our own ignorance, erroneous assumptions, insecurities, and personal preferences. Another's welfare frequently depends on my willingness to leave them alone. Next time you're tempted to fix somebody, heed these holy warnings: Do not disturb! Keep your distance! Let them be!

There is amazing grace and real blessing and ultimate kindness in keeping our hands/suggestions/towels/water to ourselves. Please do not touch the turtles!

Turtle Knows Best

The turtles will crawl back into the water when they are ready.
—A SIGN IN TURTLE COVE, OAHU

Within every human being resides a deep-seated and natural desire to make a difference in this world, to leave other people and all creation in better shape than we found them. In order to make such a difference, we set aside our own sense of time and space, stepping out of our own elements into the elements of those we are trying to help, understand, or save. For a brief moment, we look beyond what we think we know, what we assume is timely, what we perceive as truth, moving across the boundaries of theological, philosophical, and political understandings, and embracing those

166 · THE GOSPEL ACCORDING TO SAM

of another. Our primary mission and basic calling in this life is
that of reconciliation. In the New Testament, the root of that
word is to "make other," to "become other," to exchange hearts,
minds, places, or shells with one another, so that we might begin
to understand. Often, when we are there, in their space and abid-
ing in their time, we discover that we are the ones transformed,
changed, helped, empowered, and even saved. Saved from ourselves. Saved from others.

Timing is everything in the realm of God's plan and purpose,
but neither the time nor the place belongs to us. It is not our lot
to dictate a schedule, plan an itinerary of transformation, or map
out a specific location for salvation. In the meantime, there is
someone who needs our undivided attention. We are charged
with, as the Apostle Paul writes, "working out our own salvation."
That is a full-time job. So those without sin may pour the first
bottle. Those without sand may wave the first towel. But those
without flippers should not try to teach the sea creature how to
swim, and those without shells may not want to burden those who
already have one.

The turtles will go back into the water when *they* are ready. It is
not our call. It is God's, and theirs. So, please don't touch the
turtles even if you think you're just trying to help. Be touched by
them. Enjoy them. Behold them. Leave them alone. Let them be
what they are, where they are, when they choose.

Perhaps someday we will put away our watches and weapons,
our beach towels and bottled water, our plans and prejudices, our
ignorance and agendas, and we will observe true turtle time. On
that day:

Barry will sing.
Rains will cease.
Flowers will bloom.

And the voice of the turtle will be heard in all the land.

CHAPTER 29

••••••••••••

Whale Yes

Change Your Attitude, but Remain Neutral
—THE STUPA OF ENLIGHTENMENT, GAMPO ABBEY, NOVA SCOTIA

Two of my favorite names for musicians are "Hell Yeah" Smalley and Hank Snow. Decades ago I used to chow down at the Mexicatessen on Old Market Square in Houston to hear the elderly I. H. Smalley blow the hell out of a horn, step back, and shout "Hell Yeah!" to the delight of the tequila-laden crowd. In the true spirit of improvisation after any original riff by every member of his combo, Mr. Smalley would nod like a dashboard dog and bellow his appreciative affirmation to what had just transpired musically. It's amazing how much "Hell Yeah" begins to sound like "Amen" after a couple margaritas, and the spiritual sentiment is virtually synonymous. Let all God's children say, "Hell Yeah!" And if there is a better name for a Canadian country-western singer than Hank Snow, I'm not familiar with it. His two best-known songs, "Movin' On" and "I've Been Everywhere," served as musical themes for my trek around his native Nova Scotia a few years back. Inclement weather, unforeseen opportunities, and the call of the unknown kept me moving right on down the road at a most unpredictable pace. In the end, I'd pretty much been just about everywhere, including some places I'm still not even sure were there.

It was on a boat out of Westport on Brier Island at the southernmost tip of the Digby Neck that I first laid eyes on a whale named Foggy, a majestic creature aptly named after a journey so overcast I could not see the two ferries I had to board to get there. Dreary does not begin to describe the conditions under which Foggy and I met, but in such circumstances much of spiritual transformation occurs. We perceive things differently when our vision is limited, paying more attention to the signs that might be barely visible, the frequently unnoticed images that may lead to our very salvation. My eventual discovery of Foggy the whale symbolizes important spiritual truths such as the affirmation of improvisation epitomized by the "hell yeah" of the unexpected riff or unforeseen harmony and the payoff for movin' on despite threatening skies and overcast conditions. There are times when the rainbow never appears and the storm is followed by such unpleasantness as mold, mud, and terrible inconvenience. When the fog rolls in and the rain falls down, we may have no choice but to cease our fruitless search, turn off the engine, and listen. Or if we keep movin' on, we may finally arrive at a place we never knew existed, because we did not linger at the prior destination of choice. Either way, one learns to pay attention in the fog.

Don't Be So Predictable
—THE STUPA OF ENLIGHTENMENT, GAMPO ABBEY, NOVA SCOTIA

My expedition through Nova Scotia began on a drizzly August morning. Fortified by a breakfast of coffee and beaver tail (a delicious, fried pastry resembling a rodent's posterior and drenched in maple), I headed to St. Paul's Anglican Church, the oldest Protestant place of worship in Canada. I believe it was Jung, but it could have been Dr. Ruth or even Mr. Ed, who said that most sexual issues are, at root, spiritual, and most spiritual issues are, at their core, sexual. Over time, I have learned not to be surprised at the various sexual/spiritual switcheroos that frequently occur on one's search for meaning and understanding. So, I was nonplussed when Sarah the student docent abruptly switched from her dry descriptions of historic stained glass, wooden plaques, royal pews, and coats of arms, to wetter pastures. She vividly described her favorite pubs in Halifax, a city that claims to have the highest number of bars per capita in North America. How Sarah knew I was more interested in drinking than ecclesiastical history, I will never know. The rector interrupted her as he and I engaged in brief theological banter, after which Sarah did not miss a beat, resuming her ranking of preferred watering holes. She confided that she and her cousin frequently drank free or received significant student discounts "because we're pretty." I was happy to hear of her healthy sense of self-esteem but was more intrigued by her personal warning of a notorious club called the Palace. "Just be careful there," she implored. "It's the kind of place where forty-year-old men try to hit on me." I feigned horror and assured her that I could hold my own around such perverts.

Although intrigued by the scene at the Palace, I decided to spend my evening at a bar named Pacifico. Pacifico by the Atlántico, a further testimony to the attraction to the distant reality and our longing for the faraway figments of our imagination. While there I downed several flavorful local brews, such as Alexander Keith's Pale Ale (legend has it that Keith taught Sam Adams how to brew beer), while the locals demonstrated an overwhelming preference for Corona. I have observed similar beer-drinking phenomena across the globe. Locals will eschew far better regional brews in favor of some exotic, not-from-around-here cerveza even if it tastes like tap water. The beer is always better on the other side, right? Wrong! You may recall Jesus' first miracle at the wedding in Cana of Galilee where he turned water into wine. If Jesus could only turn American lagers into actual beer, I'd be much stronger in my own belief. Nevertheless, despite my cool factor diminishing in the eyes of the locals, I stuck to my suds. Had I wanted a Pacifico experience, I'd have gone to Cabo.

Don't Transfer the Ox's Load to the Cow
—THE STUPA OF ENLIGHTENMENT, GAMPO ABBEY, NOVA SCOTIA

I left Halifax and headed south early the next morning. Through the fog I could sense an endless series of tiny fishing villages, vintage wooden boats, pristine bays, historic churches, deserted beaches, and unspoiled scenery that made much of New England look like a Wal-Mart parking lot. I had planned a kayak trip around the blue waters of Mahone Bay, but the weather did not permit. Forced yet again to engage in indoor activities, I inquired at the kayak shop about my options. The young sailor strongly suggested a pub up the road in Lunenberg called the Knot. That night, the waitress at the Knot in Lunenberg unequivocally endorsed a great pub back in Mahone Bay.

On my way to Lunenberg, I passed the restaurant with the most unappetizing name of all time, the Krispy Kraut. Having lost my appetite, I settled on an ice cream cone for dinner. It was at the ice cream parlor that I met Maggie and her sister, who I pegged as two girls just out of college on a Canadian road trip. We struck up a conversation about ice cream toppings, and Maggie agreed to meet up with me later at the Knot.

I was surprised when they both walked into the Knot around 10:30 accompanied by an older man, older even than I. Geez, these girls waste no time, do they? He turned out to be their dad. Maggie, I soon discovered, was nineteen and just out of military school. Her sister wasn't old enough to drive. I believe it was Gomer Pyle from her home state of North Carolina, who put it best, "Surprise. Surprise. Surprise." Or did he say "Shazam!" Either response would have sufficed.

Margaret Elizabeth McNamara was a five-foot, one-inch package of pure sexual energy. She lived by the beach where she slept until noon, surfed for a couple of hours, and hung out with her rockstar boyfriend, the leader of a band called the Mullets, or some other hip overture toward southern culture. For the next hour and a half, especially after her father left to escort her little sister back to the hotel, Maggie and I had a most enlightening conversation, a spiritual encounter according to Jung. She had a body that was a cross between a gymnast and a swimsuit model, a winged tattoo on the far extremities of her lower back that included the words "One Love," a ruby nose piercing, and blue thong underwear that perfectly matched her eyes. I knew these things because she pointed them all out to me. She explained her tattoos: "We're all into some sexual pain thing, we just need to figure out which one. For me, it's tattoos. I'm having them all removed and then re-done." I needed another beer. A Corona. On the rocks. Drawing closer to me, she went on to review her anatomical history. "I had a breast reduction when I was fourteen—four-and-a-half pounds of breast removed. Can you believe it, William, aren't they beautiful?" Actually I could not believe it, but Lord help my unbelief. She was wearing a very low-cut, flimsy white blouse that revealed a significant portion of, well, perfection. "Quit smiling, William, your teeth turn me on," she told me. I hadn't realized I was smiling. I had thought I was only drooling.

"I want to kiss you, but my dad will tell my boyfriend." She then revealed that she and her boyfriend were "swingers." She offered to visit me in Texas if I sent her an airline ticket, but I'd have to set up her boyfriend with "a really hot girl." I did not inquire as to whether I'd have to pay the boyfriend's airfare as well.

At midnight, against Maggie's protests, her father took her away and I never saw her again. I am not sure whether to quote Pyle, Snow, or Smalley. Golly. Movin' On. Hell Yeah. All I know is, ice cream parlors are very dangerous places. I'm sticking to bars.

Don't Try to Be the Fastest
—THE STUPA OF ENLIGHTENMENT, GAMPO ABBEY, NOVA SCOTIA

The gloomy skies precluded a brief stop to surf as I headed south. Rumor had it that during hurricane season the waves there exceed ten feet (six feet American, of course). I found a surf shop just outside Liverpool on St. Catherine's River Road. I hoped to purchase a "Surf Nova Scotia" cap but entrepreneurs had yet to tap into that market. The surfer dude in residence told me that I was pretty much wasting my time in southern Nova Scotia and should've headed north where it's "way better." He acknowledged his own bias against home, admitting, "but I'm from around here." Time up north might change his perspective.

The rain offered a good excuse to hang out a little longer in Liverpool. At the Hank Snow Museum, appropriately located in an old train depot, I asked the young girl taking tickets which album was the best. She tried to pawn off some canned Nashville country and flimsy Canadian pop. She was obviously no friend of Hank. I decided that the Doobie Brothers would complement Snow's northern drawl. Besides, "Jesus Is Just All Right with Me."

Quirky little Liverpool is known for its photography museum. I ducked into a local department store to purchase some rain gear, the bright yellow heavy-duty kind I wore in grade school, the kind you can't find anymore. I asked the lady behind the counter about the photography museum. She made a sweeping gesture toward the outside of the store and confided, "You know, I've never been there, but I hear it's that way." The ignorance of the familiar was, by then, a familiar theme. The photography museum was right across the street.

The photographer Sherman Hines seems to be best known for his dramatic nature photography (foggy piers, striking seascapes, soaring coastlines). I found his outhouse series much more compelling. The unique aesthetics and contextual architecture of such utilitarian spaces inspired me. I bought three prints, feeling they would look lovely next to the historic pictures of Canterbury Cathedral hanging in my office.

My conversation with the young female docents suddenly shifted from light, balance, and lack of outdoor plumbing to local taverns. Honestly, I am not sure how this happened. The docents urged me to head back to Halifax where it was "so much cooler." One of them proceeded to describe the Liverpool nightlife as consisting of two possibilities: Dooley's, a "pool hall with a disco ball," and the grill at the bowling alley where you can find Fisherman's Karaoke on Sundays. "Five-hundred-pound fishermen prance around with their butt cracks showing singing Britney Spears songs. I have *not* been back!" the young girl testified. I was sad that it was Monday. Had it been Sunday, I'd have spent the night.

As I drove the length of the Digby Neck early the next morning, through East Ferry, Iverton, Freeport, and finally to Westport on Brier Island, the whole world seemed to be shrouded in mist. I was surrounded by scenic landscapes but could not see them. Finding the ferry entrance was a leap of faith. I could only assume the car ahead of me was driving on to some sort of solid floating terrain instead of plunging into the abyss of the sea. I had picked a perfect day to watch whales! I wondered what sort of indoor activities are favored by large seafaring mammals. Do humpbacks frequent taverns?

I chose for my whale-watching expedition an old wooden vessel owned and operated by the Graham family. It traveled more slowly, but the nature of my journey seemed to rule out the efficiency of a Zodiac. What was the rush exactly? I had made the right choice. Mrs. Graham offered the passengers home-baked muffins and potent hot chocolate. Mr. Graham proved an able captain. The deckhand provided comic relief by eating krill, a species of tiny, briny, floating whale food. There was even a naturalist aboard to answer our weightier questions.

Before leaving the dock, Mrs. Graham clearly stated that if we were the type of people who are in a big hurry, demand instant gratification, and desire a money-back guarantee, we'd come to the wrong boat. Spotting a whale takes time, patience, and some luck. The chances were pretty good that we'd see one, but not at all certain. I had seen the marketing ploys of other whale cruises offering full refunds if the customer was not completely satisfied. Such an approach seemed unethical, unecological, and all washed up to me. The Grahams had it right. Whale-watching is a fine lesson about our lack of control, and about how we find most of the breathtakingly important stuff in this life: meaning, beauty, fulfillment, love, and even God. We take our chances by entering the mystery.

Although the fog was patchier offshore, visibility was still limited to a football field or less. We spent a great deal of time with the engine off, drifting aimlessly, listening intently. During this time, Mrs. Graham told us to stuff a muffin in our mouths and pay attention. If that isn't a metaphor for a necessary spiritual discipline, then I'll eat krill. Turn off the engine. Drift aimlessly. Listen intently. You might hear something important, a sound to set you on the right path. We listened a long time, until some sort of cetacean tune was heard, and the captain headed in that direction.

In order for onlookers to see the tail of a whale, the most balletic and breathtaking of this big mammal's movements, the whale has to dive deep, to depart from the surface, to leave the premises. What that means is, to get a glimpse of the good stuff one has to be willing to say *sayonara*: "Ladies and gentlemen, Foggy has left the building." The whale will disappear underneath the surface and may not be spotted again. I have seen whales swim along the surface, plow the seas like fullbacks, and rhythmically rotate like giant torpedos; but the very first time I saw a whale, it was the tail working its magic through the fog.

It was hazy and distant and fleeting, but luminous, stunning, and magical. I had no words to describe such a vision, until a man standing next to me excitedly shouted to his wife, "Did you see that?" Oblivious to the fact that he was not speaking to me and touched by the moment of transcendence, exhilarated by this awesome sight, I blurted the unmistakably extraordinary truth. "Hell yeah!" I had meant to say, "Amen."

Don't Expect Applause
—THE STUPA OF ENLIGHTENMENT, GAMPO ABBEY, NOVA SCOTIA

Days later in Pleasant Bay on the northwest tip of Cape Breton, a large, bright spherical object finally appeared in the sky. For the first time since I'd set foot on the soil of New Scotland, there was no moisture in the air or haze on the horizon. It was a perfect day for whale-watching, so I decided to savor the glorious conditions and embark on another excursion. The captain of the Pleasant Bay boat was a sweet, weathered fellow, a retired fisherman, who called me up into the cab to get warm and dry. On a clear day with unlimited visibility, I had gotten drenched by the seas and had my appendages nearly frozen off by a bitter wind. We spotted just one pilot whale from a great distance, but the trip was salvaged by the sight of seals, the "dogs of the sea." Given the stellar performance I witnessed, "hams of the sea" may more aptly describe them. Apart from the antics of the sea dogs, it was a rather boring cruise. Sunny skies and open vistas can make for monotony as often as meaning.

Whale-watching in the fog was much more intriguing. A little mystery, unknown, and otherness piques our curiosity and heightens our awareness on the seas and in the spiritual dimension. When things seem perfectly clear, we are probably confused. Uncertainty and surprise frequently accompany spiritual depth. When it's the real deal, we may glimpse but a tail. Truth dives deep and tends to disappear. Surrounded by fog, barely visible in the haze, ultimate reality looms large—if we're paying attention. So, turn off the engine. Drift a while. Listen with all of your heart and most of your ears.

The kindly captain encouraged me to take a hike that afternoon toward Pallett's Cove where his grandfather owned land for more than a century, and to stop by the Buddhist monastery at the end of the trail, promising that the "monks would be glad to see you." So I hiked the trail that day and found the monastery, Gampo Abbey. The monks were nowhere to be seen, praying in isolation, I presume. But a white-tailed fox darted from the darkness of the woods to welcome me as I drew near to the Stupa of Enlightenment, a sort of Buddhist representation of spiritual knowledge. Around the stupa were fifty-nine spiritual slogans. Some of my favorites were: "Change your attitude, but remain neutral. Don't be so predictable. Don't transfer the ox's load to the cow. Don't try to be the fastest. Don't expect applause."

I returned from Nova Scotia with a beer mug from the Alexander Keith's Brewery, a multicolored whale tail from a small art gallery near Mabou, a copy of Hank Snow's *Greatest Hits* CD, and a ticket stub from the Save Our Shores concert in Cape Breton.

The concert featured uplifting Celtic tunes and a series of jokes about Texas. The purpose of the musical fundraiser was to stop seismic testing, a prelude to oil and gas exploration just off the coast, for fear that it might harm the whales and other creatures of the deep. I reminded myself that my people were in Scotland before they were in Texas, and the whales were here long before any of us. I returned also with a new appreciation for the art of improvisation, and the value of movin' on. Everywhere. For there is much to see, especially in the fog.

CHAPTER 30

....

Bunny Hop

I believe it was James Thurber who said, "Love is what you've been through with someone." Old Sam and I have been through a lot over these past eleven years. We should seriously consider a reality TV show, perhaps something like: *Survivors: The Dog Days of Spring, Summer, and Fall.*

In the spring of Sam's life, his eyes were filled with wonder, and new discoveries were made every day. I was blessed to begin a new ministry at a historically African American congregation in Austin, where my world was expanded and my life greatly enriched. But even as a puppy, Sam experienced the gas leak, explosion, and fire that cost him his ears and nearly his life. Being barely thirty, I buried my mother on All Saints' Day. The flowers got watered, and the bloom was on more often than off, but spring sprang a leak every now and then.

What fun we had in summertime as Sam learned to swim, wrestle, play tug-of-war, and fetch the fluffy man. He fine-tuned his negotiating skills for food, began to recognize the supreme value of Texas barbeque, and flaunted his golden locks and teddy-bear charm to endear himself to the multitudes. Sam became a minor celebrity in Austin where everyone knew his name and what he had been through. Of course, even in the summer there were ear infections and stomach upsets, cat paws to contend with, and a near-fatal collision with a car in front of his home. Life was never merely a bed of dog biscuits. My dabbling in music, acting, and modeling were interesting diversions that reinforced the fact that I should not quit my day job. Life continued to happen while I made other plans. Willie Nelson, I'm not. My thespian tendencies relate more to childhood trauma than raw talent, and Calvin Klein never returned my call. My theory that there should be at least one potbellied underwear model was never embraced by the culture at large.

It is now fall, and the changes happen with alarming frequency. Or do I just now notice what has been creeping up on us over the years, like the day one suddenly realizes that one's parents have grown old? Sam's eyes still sparkle, but they reveal more wisdom than discovery. He looks around like a distinguished judge rather than a rascal up to no good. Just when Sam was slowing down to the pace of an inanimate object and achieving the attitude of a grumpy canine codger, little Jack arrived from Oklahoma and gave Sam a second wind, a new leash on life. While Sam may not engage in a game of chase or romp through the fields full throttle in pursuit of his little brother, he will defend his tail should it get chomped, and participate in cable TV–caliber body slams should Jack initiate trouble. He has found his voice again, engaging in bark-offs at the slightest provocation. Not irritating shrill yaps, mind you, but deep woofs of wisdom that seem to say, "I have spoken—just kidding."

Sam is not getting any younger, and neither am I. Time takes its toll on all creation. Some little amoeba nearly killed him not long ago. Our good friend and veterinarian Dr. Valerie McDaniel took one look at my nearly lifeless shriveled-up lump of sickness and spent a whole week pumping him full of fluids and antibiotics. Thanks to the kindness of others, the wonders of medicine, and my clergy discount, once again, Sam survived. Recently Sam had a couple of tumors removed, a small one that interrupted a favorite scratching spot on his chest and a monster that had wrapped itself all the way around his big toe. Dr. McDaniel was concerned about removing the affected toe, but I assured her that if Sam didn't eat with it or sleep on it, he'd never know the difference. Sam is now the fearless, earless, toeless Airedale. The absence of some minor appendage isn't about to stop Sam.

My personal autumn began when my father passed away just as he was hoping to begin a new chapter in his life. Some say that you don't become an adult until you've lost both of your parents. I suppose that one is all grown up when there is no more permanent address to fill out on forms, and no one in particular to call when there is good or bad news that simply must be shared. My ambitions to become a hot-shot rector in the Big Apple or a Southern California party priest were thwarted when the Big Dog had other plans. I became rector of historic, inner-city Trinity Church in Houston. Even when in Austin with his mom, Sam is only a short commute away and so immediately sent his letter of transfer to the parish administrator. He's the best greeter we've got and has somehow managed to get himself preserved for posterity in a modern stained-glass window in the Morrow Chapel. The window is dedicated to a beloved pediatrician who died shortly after my arrival. Sam anchors the children's corner where he peers from behind the Holy Spirit along with Dr. Moore's finger puppets and long-cherished pup. His paw holds down the diversity ribbon as it weaves its way among the symbols of God's varied presence in our lives. I am home, and I am happy. Mostly. Even though the Astros still can't win even with Roger Clemens. Come October, I fear they will have dropped in the standings faster than the leaves from the trees. One learns a lot about anticipating the next season from following the 'Stros.

As the seasons unfold, it is evermore apparent that the gospel according to Sam is mostly about wagging one's tail through adversity, surviving and thriving in season and out. It has more to do with survival than celebrity; scars are more revealing than stars. When we are asked about ultimate meaning, happiness, and success, we cannot point to the trophy case, garage, bank account, or dog show ribbons. We can only lift our shirts, hike up our pants, part our fur, or motion toward some internal organ like the heart, showing our scars, that we have survived. The sharing of such stories is the sharing of the gospel; more potent than untested beauty, more holy than painted-on perfection, more true than the thin clichés of popular religion.

The cool breeze of autumn is welcome relief from the oppressive Gulf Coast heat. But such winds remind me that winter will be here too soon. My buddy is an old man now. I make such an observation with great respect and no hint of judgment. I am fully aware that, in dog years, I'm already dead.

In these pretwilight times, not yet dusk, but cool enough to sit on the porch before the sun goes down, I am pained by every missed step or dulled sense. Sam doesn't always hear the dogs calling from next door or the door opening when I return home. These days, he cannot quite see the highly nuanced details of life on the outside, life still keenly taken in by that sharp-sighted Jack. He can no longer leap into the shotgun seat of my truck in a single bound, and sometimes he needs help even if the lower floor board is available as an intermediate step. Occasionally he will get a running start and attempt to scale the passengerial heights. Almost always he misses, and slips right back onto the pavement below. I have found that a firm hand on his bony backside and a slight shove in an upward direction does wonders for his forward movement.

Sam boldly attempts any rung of stairs, regardless of the incline level or surface surety. More than once I've watched him slide down back to where he began, unintentionally belly surfing backwards. My heart sinks at the sight of such setbacks, but Sam will not be deterred. Even during this most telling manifestation of the aging process, his ongoing difficulty with climbing stairs, Sam has persevered and discovered a way to get where he wants to be. Unintimidated and undeterred by his painful arthritis and uncooperative hip, Sam does whatever it takes to scale the heights. When it hurts too much to climb, Sam does what any determined dog would do. He bunny hops. All the way to the top.

The animal authorities tell us that such bunny-hop behavior is typical for dogs with hip problems. Many of us would simply take the elevator and resign ourselves to a lifetime of lateral movement, but not Sam. Just because it isn't easy does not preclude the attempt. His efforts encourage me and teach me about adaptation, perseverance, and determination.

I sat at my computer in my upstairs study on a December afternoon, writing my Christmas Eve sermon and thinking about the theology of incarnation. When God wanted to communicate ultimate love, God dared descend to our level to be with us, even as a child born in a manger. Of all biblical theologies, it is perhaps my favorite, and of all religious services, Christmas Eve remains my personal preference. There is something extraordinary and holy about that night and that truth, so personal and real and unlikely. At this moment of intense contemplation on the mystery of incarnation I heard a slow, steady movement beginning at the bottom of the stairs, and I realized that soon I would not be alone. *Ph-thump. Ph-thump. Ph-thump.* Slowly, gradually, painfully, hoppily, Sam ascended every stair. There were no delicious pork ribs in the study, no cool new toys to play with, no dainty French poodles to ogle. It was just me up there that afternoon. Sam made all that effort—simply to be with me. He drew near looking winded, but his tail shouted "Glory to God in the Highest!" and danced back and forth like a trumpeter from the Grambling Band. I stopped my research and embraced my best friend, understanding in that moment the theology of incarnation. Sam with me. God with us. Bunny hop as sacred movement and painful sacrifice, leading us toward a higher plane of living and being, together at last with ultimate love.

As Sam has gotten older, he acts out more of his dreams. When he is lying down, typically sideways, I detect a more active and vivid dream-state and a more embodied manifestation of his imagination. He seems to be dreaming of racing, jumping, or leaping. He appears to be galloping like a thoroughbred racehorse. His body language is so pronounced that he often makes enough noise to awaken me from sleep or distract me from whatever task I'm engaged in. Sometimes I stand over him and watch as he pounds the pavement, all cylinders thrusting on all four paws, every leg gracefully bounding, even those back bunny hoppers moving with a fluidlike rhythm, faster and faster and faster. Perhaps, in his dream, he is winning the Kentucky Derby, galloping up a mile of stairs to light the Olympic torch, or outrunning Jack in a race to the barbeque pit. Or perhaps he is just humping the dog down the street. Either way, his imagination soars, and he seems to be having a very good time. The bunny hops are long-forgotten in this mystical land of majestic leaps. One is never too old to dream, and even to embrace and embody those visions.

As I have aged, it appears that Sam and I have even more in common. I have come to appreciate the value of frequent naps, and the possibility of sleeping twenty hours a day no longer seems like a waste of time. I've slowed down, too. I now prefer baseball to basketball. It's better for the consumption of beer, the digestion of hot dogs, and the possibility of conversation. Hangovers are more frequent after less alcohol. I have to take a sick day after excessive partying. What used to be the wee hours are now the pee hours as I see more of my restroom before dawn than I thought possible. Longer workouts achieve fewer physical results. I forget where I parked or who the girl is whose number I've programmed into my cell phone. Sitting on the porch and feeling the wind actually generates a thrill. When confronted with stairs, I contemplate alternate modes of transportation. Bunnies have less to do with Hef and more to do with Bugs. And, as with Sam, the chase is still exciting, but mostly in my dreams.

Still, as I've aged, I'd like to think I've gained some sense of perspective. I'd hope to possess a little more wisdom and understanding about what matters than I had on the other side of the womb. But increased understanding does not entail trading my sense of irreverence for irrelevance.

Even though Sam sometimes assumes the posture of a seasoned sage and looks right on past my exterior to the empty spaces in my soul, he still possesses the personality of a prankster. He is more selective about how he expends his energy and time, but his grin can still broaden to mischief-size as he playfully works the room, doing his Chewbacca imitation to draw a laugh, lying on his back with paws extended to get your attention, woofing loudly, and flouncing around on the floor if he feels that things have gotten way too serious. Serial solemnity is a sure sign that the Spirit has left the room, choosing to find a more entertaining venue.

Down at the Tiki Island bay house, which Sam, Jack, and I share with two couples, a baby, and five dogs, one may witness what could be misconstrued as immature antics which are, in fact, telltale signs of the living, laughing Spirit of God. My friend Michael and his wife Andrea just had a baby, Perri. Michael loves to put his favorite purple pimp hat on Perri and hum the theme from *Shaft* to coax him to sleep. Michael takes his responsibilities as a dad quite seriously, but that doesn't stop him from engaging in ridiculously sublime behavior. We keep a large basket of stuffed dog toys in the corner of the bay house living room. The dogs may freely choose any toy at any time: the snake, the helicopter, the duck, the bone. One day, Michael snatched up his personal favorite, the beaver, and sensing a captive audience, instructed all of us to watch him. He faced away from us, hid the beaver from view, and spread his legs apart. Making loud, realistic, forceful birthing noises, he lowered the beaver between his legs, and we saw it fall to the floor. He then gasped a sigh of relief. It's one of those sight gags you have to see and hear to fully appreciate, but we, possessing similarly warped senses of humor, laughed hard. Upon regaining my composure, I told him in serious tones, "Michael, we always suspected there was a beaver between your legs." The banter of juveniles? Or the fruits of the Spirit? Or both?

Spiritual maturity has nothing to do with solemn looks and musty old approaches to religion that maintain the boundaries of taste. Lifeless and tired, such a spirituality is in need of some sort of spiritual Viagra. Wisdom retains a sense of humor and develops a sense of perspective. When Sam ceases the Chewbacca, the roll-over, the floor-stomp, and the galloping dreams; when there are no more grins, drool, sniffs, or nudges between my legs, I will begin to worry. But for now, his heart still beats, his tail still wags, his soul still sings.

Spiritual wisdom retains all the fun with one-third more perspective. We laugh hard, but think harder. We dare to ask deep questions and seek the big picture. What is important? What really lasts? What ultimately matters? What will I leave behind? Growing old gracefully is to ponder such things, all the while giving birth to beavers among friends.

According to Sam, the wisdom of the ages has nothing to do with what we retain: ears, toes, wealth, success, certainty. It has everything to do with what we give away. According to Sam, there is only one thing that can transcend every season and outlast us all, that would bunny hop all the way up the stairs and over the top. Even to the very end.

It is the love of a faithful friend.

A Postscript on Love

Not long after I wrote the final chapter of Sam's book, little Jack decided to add his own postscript on love. One day in Austin, as Rachel set off for work, she attached Jack's bark collar so that he would not disturb the peace. Jack's ability to vocalize at the decibel level of a sonic boom was well known throughout the neighborhood. Jack, being a quick study, figured out after a single zap that when the bark collar goes on, the trap stays shut. So during the day when Rachel was away, Jack went on a silent retreat. The audible sounds emanating from Rachel's apartment from 9 to 5, Monday through Friday, resembled those from a monastery at bedtime; that is, until Sam got into some serious trouble.

Time continued to take its toll on old Sam, reducing his ability to engage in upward movement and forward progression. On this particular day, Sam had somehow maneuvered into a favorite napping spot under Rachel's bed. However, when snack time arrived and he tried to come up for food, his back legs completely gave out on him. He got stuck, and no amount of flailing on the floor or banging his head on the box springs could set him free. Sam panicked and began to whimper in helpless, heartfelt cries, mostly unheard underneath the great mattress barrier.

When Jack heard Sam's pleas, he would not let them go unheeded. Bark collar or not, Jack howled his distress in alarming, urgent tones, attempting to alert the neighbors that Sam was in dire straits and needed immediate help. Jack pleaded so loudly that Karen, the downstairs neighbor, knew something was terribly wrong, raced up to Rachel's apartment, and rescued Sam from his bedtime bondage.

I seriously doubt that Jack could even begin to understand the intricacies of motivating factors or articulate particular thought processes related to his heroic behavior, but I am quite certain that Sam was saved that day by the power of love. If faith reveals anything, it is that love will endure pain and suffering and will overcome every obstacle and predicament on behalf of the object of its affection. This love is selfless, brave, loyal, and true. Indeed, it is downright shocking how far such love will go when our friends are in need or trouble.

The torch was passed, and none too soon. The week we were scheduled to go to print with this book, Sam developed serious breathing problems. Fearing some sort of tumor or scar tissue from the long-ago fire or that he had developed adult-onset asthma like his dad, we immediately took him in for a check-up. Sam's wonderful veterinarian, Dr. Valerie McDaniel, seemed visibly sad as she showed me his x-ray. "Here's the problem," she said as she pointed toward his heart. "Sam's heart is more than twice the size of a normal heart." We had always suspected as much.

Three days later Rachel drove to Houston to be with him. We surrounded Sam for hours with tangible expressions of our love: pillows, hugs, scratches, kisses, and cheese. He reciprocated with several face-licks of his own. We told litanies of Sam stories, whispered various affections in his ear, and cried dog bowls of tears. Just when things were getting a little too solemn, Sam let go with one last poop. It was the last time I saw his tail fully erect.

His breathing was shallow and his body was weak. Though heavily sedated, his eyes still sparkled and looked longingly at each of us—knowingly, affectionately, lovingly. In fact, whenever either Rachel or I would momentarily get up and wander away from the sacred scene, even for a moment, Sam would lift his head off the pillow in an attempt to track us down. Of course, his head also popped up whenever the refrigerator door would open.

Near the end, I bawled my way through an animal prayer of committal, thanksgiving, and hope. Dr. McDaniel and her husband Mack, our good friend Steve, and Rachel and I placed our hands over Sam's big heart. At 10:00 p.m. on August 26, 2005, Sam closed his eyes and breathed his last breath.

Later on, I checked my church calendar to see if August 26 might be the feast day of some significant or even lesser known saint. No one's name appeared. Apparently the day remains unclaimed. That is, until now.

CPSIA information can be obtained
at www.ICGtesting.com
Printed in the USA
FSOW03n2150110717
36033FS